W9-CMM-291

The Digestive System

Regina Avraham

Introduction by C. Everett Koop, M.D., Sc.D.
Former Surgeon General, U.S. Public Health Service

Foreword by Sandra Thurman
Director, Office of National AIDS Policy, The White House

CHELSEA HOUSE PUBLISHERS
Philadelphia

The goal of the 21ST CENTURY HEALTH AND WELLNESS is to provide general information in the ever-changing areas of physiology, psychology, and related medical issues. The titles in this series are not intended to take the place of the professional advice of a physician or other health-care professional.

COVER PHOTOS: Burger & Ginger courtesy of Emiliano Begnardi

Chelsea House Publishers
EDITOR IN CHIEF: Stephen Reginald
MANAGING EDITOR: James D. Gallagher
PRODUCTION MANAGER: Pam Loos
ART DIRECTOR: Sara Davis
DIRECTOR OF PHOTOGRAPHY: Judy Hasday
SENIOR PRODUCTION EDITOR: Lee Anne Gelletly
ASSISTANT EDITOR: Anne Hill
PRODUCTION SERVICES: Pre-Press Company, Inc.
COVER DESIGNER/ILLUSTRATOR: Emiliano Begnardi

The Chelsea House World Wide Web site address is http://www.chelseahouse.com

3 5 7 9 8 6 4 2

Library of Congress Cataloging-in-Publication Data

Avraham, Regina.
Digestive System / Regina Avraham.
p.   cm. — (21st century health and wellness)
Includes bibliographical references and index.
Summary: An overview of the digestive system and how it works.
ISBN 0-7910-5526-4
1. Digestion—Juvenile literature. 2. Gastrointestinal system — Physiology—Juvenile literature. [1. Digestive System.] I. Title. II. Series.

QP145.A97 1999
612.3—dc21

99-047869

CONTENTS

- **AIDS**
- **Allergies**
- **The Circulatory System**
- **The Digestive System**
- **The Immune System**
- **Mononucleosis and Other Infectious Diseases**
- **Organ Transplants**
- **Pregnancy & Birth**
- **The Respiratory System**
- **Sexually Transmitted Diseases**
- **Sports Medicine**

PREVENTION AND EDUCATION: THE KEYS TO GOOD HEALTH

C. Everett Koop, M.D., Sc.D.
FORMER SURGEON GENERAL,
U.S. Public Health Service

The issue of health education has received particular attention in recent years because of the presence of AIDS in the news. But our response to this particular tragedy points up a number of broader issues that doctors, public health officials, educators, and the public face. In particular, it spotlights the importance of sound health education for citizens of all ages.

Over the past 35 years, this country has been able to achieve dramatic declines in the death rates from heart disease, stroke, accidents, and—for people under the age of 45—cancer. Today, Americans generally eat better and take better care of themselves than ever before. Thus, with the help of modern science and technology, they have a better chance of surviving serious—even catastrophic—illnesses. In 1996, the life expectancy of Americans reached an all-time high of 76.1 years. That's the good news.

The flip side of this advance has special significance for young adults. According to a report issued in 1998 by the U.S. Department of Health and Human Services, levels of wealth and education in the United States are directly correlated with our population's health. The more money Americans make and the more years of schooling they have, the better their health will be. Furthermore, income inequality increased in the U.S. between 1970 and 1996. Basically, the rich got richer—people in high income brackets had greater increases in the amount of money made than did those at low income levels. In addition, the report indicated that children under 18 are more likely to live in poverty than the population as a whole.

Family income rises with each higher level of education for both men and women from every ethnic and racial background. Life expectancy, too, is related to family income. People with lower incomes tend to die at younger ages than people from more affluent homes. What all this means is that health is a factor of wealth and education, both of which need to be improved for all Americans if the promise of life, liberty, and the pursuit of happiness is to include an equal chance for good health.

The health of young people is further threatened by violent death and injury, alcohol and drug abuse, unwanted pregnancies, and sexually transmitted diseases. Adolescents are particularly vulnerable because they are beginning to explore their own sexuality and perhaps to experiment with drugs and alcohol. We need to educate young people to avoid serious dangers to their health. The price of neglect is high.

Even for the population as a whole, health is still far from what it could be. Why? Most death and disease are attributed to four broad elements: inadequacies in the health-care system, behavioral factors or unhealthy lifestyles, environmental hazards, and human biological factors. These categories are also influenced by individual resources. For example, low birth weight and infant mortality are more common among the children of less educated mothers. Likewise, women with more education are more likely to obtain prenatal care during pregnancy. Mothers with fewer than 12 years of education are almost 10 times more likely to smoke during pregnancy—and new studies find excessive aggression later in life as well as other physical ailments among the children of smokers. In short, poor people with less education are more likely to smoke cigarettes, which endangers health and shortens the life span. About a third of the children who begin smoking will eventually have their lives cut short because of this practice.

Similarly, poor children are exposed more often to environmental lead, which causes a wide range of physical and mental problems. Sedentary lifestyles are also more common among teens with lower family income than among wealthier adolescents. Being overweight—a condition associated with physical inactivity as well as excessive caloric intake—is also more common among poor, non-Hispanic, white adolescents. Children from rich families are more likely to have health insurance. Therefore, they are more apt to receive vaccinations and other forms of early preventative medicine and treatment. The bottom line is that kids from lower income groups receive less adequate health care.

To be sure, some diseases are still beyond the control of even the most advanced medical techniques that our richest citizens can afford. Despite yearnings that are as old as the human race itself, there is no "fountain of youth" to prevent aging and death. Still, solutions are available for many of the problems that undermine sound health. In a word, that solution is prevention. Prevention, which includes health promotion and education, can save lives, improve the quality of life, and, in the long run, save money.

In the United States, organized public health activities and preventative medicine have a long history. Important milestones include the improvement of sanitary procedures and the development of pasteurized milk in the late-19th century, and the introduction in the mid-20th century of effective vaccines against polio, measles, German measles, mumps, and other once-rampant diseases. Internationally, organized public health efforts began on a wide-scale basis with the International Sanitary Conference of 1851, to which 12 nations sent representatives. The World Health Organization, founded in 1948, continues these efforts under the aegis of the United Nations, with particular emphasis on combating communicable diseases and the training of health-care workers.

Despite these accomplishments, much remains to be done in the field of prevention. For too long, we have had a medical system that is science and technology-based, and focuses essentially on illness and mortality. It is now patently obvious that both the social and the economic costs of such a system are becoming insupportable.

Implementing prevention and its corollaries, health education and health promotion, is the job of several groups of people. First, the medical and scientific professions need to continue basic scientific research, and here we are making considerable progress. But increased concern with prevention will also have a decided impact on how primary-care doctors practice medicine. With a shift to health-based rather than morbidity-based medicine, the role of the "new physician" includes a healthy dose of patient education.

Second, practitioners of the social and behavioral sciences—psychologists, economists, and city planners along with lawyers, business leaders, and government officials—must solve the practical and ethical dilemmas confronting us: poverty, crime, civil rights, literacy, education, employment, housing, sanitation, environmental protection, health-care delivery systems, and so forth. All of these issues affect public health.

Third is the public at large. We consider this group to be important in any movement. Fourth, and the linchpin in this effort, is the public health profession: doctors, epidemiologists, teachers—who must harness the professional expertise of the first two groups and the common sense and cooperation of the third: the public. They must define the problems statistically and qualitatively and then help set priorities for finding solutions.

To a very large extent, improving health statistics is the responsiblity of every individual. So let's consider more specifically what the role of the individual should be and why health education is so important. First, and most obviously, individuals can protect themselves from illness and injury and thus minimize the need for professional medical care. They can eat a nutritious diet; get adequate exercise; avoid tobacco, alcohol, and drugs; and take prudent steps to avoid accidents. The proverbial "apple a day keeps the doctor away" is not so far from the truth, after all.

Second, individuals should actively participate in their own medical care. They should schedule regular medical and dental checkups. If an illness or injury develops, they should know when to treat themselves and when to seek professional help. To gain the maximum benefit from any medical treatment, individuals must become partners in treatment. For instance, they should understand the effects and side effects of medications. I counsel young physicians that there is no such thing as too much information when talking with patients. But the corollary is the patient must know enough about the nuts and bolts of the healing process to understand what the doctor is telling him or her. That responsibility is at least partially the patient's.

Education is equally necessary for us to understand the ethical and public policy issues in health care today. Sometimes individuals will encounter these issues in making decisions about their own treatment or that of family members. Other citizens may encounter them as jurors in medical malpractice cases. But we all become involved, indirectly, when we elect our public officials, from school board members to the president. Should surrogate parenting be legal? To what extent is drug testing desirable, legal, or necessary? Should there be public funding for family planning, hospitals, various types of medical research, and medical care for the indigent? How should we allocate scant technological resources, such as kidney dialysis and organ transplants? What is the proper role of government in protecting the rights of patients?

What are the broad goals of public health in the United States today? The Public Health Service has defined these goals in terms of mortality, education, and health improvement. It identified 15 major concerns: controlling high blood pressure, improving family planning, pregnancy care and infant health, increasing the rate of immunization, controlling sexually transmitted diseases, controlling the presence of toxic agents or radiation in the environment, improving occupational safety and health, preventing accidents, promoting water fluoridation and dental health, controlling infectious diseases, decreasing smoking, decreasing alcohol and drug abuse, improving nutrition, promoting physical fitness and exercise, and controlling stress and violent behavior. Great progress has been made in many of these areas. For example, the report *Health, United States, 1998* indicates that in general, the workplace is safer today than it was a decade ago. Between 1980 and 1993, the overall death rate from occupational injuries dropped 45 percent to 4.2 deaths per 100,000 workers.

For healthy adolescents and young adults (ages 15 to 24), the specific goal defined by the Public Health Service was a 20% reduction in deaths, with a special focus on motor vehicle injuries as well as alcohol and drug abuse. For adults (ages 25 to 64), the aim was 25% fewer deaths, with a concentration on heart attacks, strokes, and cancers. In the 1999 National Drug Control Strategy, the White House Office of National Drug Control Policy echoed the Congressional goal of reducing drug use by 50 percent in the coming decade.

Smoking is perhaps the best example of how individual behavior can have a direct impact on health. Today cigarette smoking is recognized as the most important single preventable cause of death in our society. It is responsible for more cancers and more cancer deaths than any other known agent; is a prime risk factor for heart and blood vessel disease, chronic bronchitis, and emphysema; and is a frequent cause of complications in pregnancies and of babies born prematurely, underweight, or with potentially fatal respiratory and cardiovascular problems.

Since the release of the Surgeon General's first report on smoking in 1964, the proportion of adult smokers has declined substantially, from 43% in 1965 to 30.5% in 1985. The rate of cigarette smoking among adults declined from 1974 to 1995, but rates of decline were greater among the more educated. Since 1965, more than 50 million people have quit smoking. Although the rate of adult smoking has decreased, children and teenagers are smoking more. Researchers have also noted a disturbing correlation between underage smoking of cigarettes and later use of cocaine and heroin. Although there is still much work to be done if we are to become a "smoke free society," it is heartening to note that public health and public education efforts—such as warnings on cigarette packages, bans on broadcast advertising, removal of billboards advertising cigarettes, and anti-drug youth campaigns in the media— have already had significant effects.

In 1997, the first leveling off of drug use since 1992 was found in eighth graders, with marijuana use in the past month declining to 10 percent. The percentage of eighth graders who drink alcohol or smoke cigarettes also decreased slightly in 1997. In 1994 and 1995, there were more than 142,000 cocaine-related emergency-room episodes per year, the highest number ever reported since these events were tracked starting in 1978. Illegal drugs present a serious threat to Americans who use these drugs. Addiction is a chronic, relapsing disease that changes the chemistry of the brain in harmful ways. The abuse of inhalants and solvents found in legal products like hair spray, paint thinner, and industrial cleaners—called "huffing" (through the mouth) or "sniffing" (through the nose)—has come to public attention in recent years. *The National Household Survey on Drug Abuse* discovered that among youngsters ages 12 to 17, this dangerous practice doubled between 1991 and 1996 from 10.3 percent to 21 percent. An alarming large number of children died the very first time they tried inhalants, which can also cause brain damage or injure other vital organs.

Another threat to public health comes from firearm injuries. Fortunately, the number of such assaults declined between 1993 and 1996. Nevertheless, excessive violence in our culture—as depicted in the mass media—may have contributed to the random shootings at Columbine High School in Littleton, Colorado, and elsewhere. The government and private citizens are rethinking how to reduce the fascination with violence so that America can become a safer, healthier place to live.

The "smart money" is on improving health care for everyone. Only recently did we realize that the gap between the "haves" and "have-nots" had a significant health component. One more reason to invest in education is that schooling produces better health.

In 1835, Alexis de Tocqueville, a French visitor to America, wrote, "In America, the passion for physical well-being is general." Today, as then, health and fitness are front-page items. But with the greater scientific and technological resources now available to us, we are in a far stronger position to make good health care available to everyone. With the greater technological threats to us as we approach the 21st century, the need to do so is more urgent than ever before. Comprehensive information about basic biology, preventative medicine, medical and surgical treatments, and related ethical and public policy issues can help you arm yourself with adequate knowledge to be healthy throughout life.

FOREWORD

Sandra Thurman, Director, Office of National AIDS Policy, The White House

A hundred years ago, an era was marked by discovery, invention, and the infinite possibilities of progress. Nothing peaked society's curiosity more than the mysterious workings of the human body. They poked and prodded, experimented with new remedies and discarded old ones, increased longevity and reduced death rates. But not even the most enterprising minds of the day could have dreamed of the advancements that would soon become our shared reality. Could they have envisioned that we would vaccinate millions of children against polio? Ward off the annoyance of allergy season with a single pill? Or give life to a heart that had stopped keeping time?

As we stand on the brink of a new millennium, the progress made during the last hundred years is indeed staggering. And we continue to push forward every minute of every day. We now exist in a working global community, blasting through cyber-space at the speed of light, sharing knowledge and up-to-the-minute technology. We are in a unique position to benefit from the world's rich fabric of traditional healing practices while continuing to explore advances in modern medicine. In the halls of our medical schools, tomorrow's healers are learning to appreciate the complexities of our whole person. We are not only keeping people alive, we are keeping them well.

Although we deserve to rejoice in our progress, we must also remember that our health remains a complex web. Our world changes with each step forward and we are continuously faced with new threats to our well-being. The air we breathe has become polluted, the water tainted, and new killers have emerged to challenge us in ways we are just beginning to understand. AIDS, in particular, continues to tighten its grip on America's most fragile communities, and place our next generation in jeopardy.

Facing these new challenges will require us to find inventive ways to stay healthy. We already know the dangers of alcohol, smoking and drug abuse. We also understand the benefits of early detection for illnesses like cancer and heart disease, two areas where scientists have made significant in-roads to treatment. We have become a well-informed society, and with that information comes a renewed emphasis on preventative care and a sense of personal responsibility to care for both ourselves and those who need our help.

Read. Re-read. Study. Explore the amazing working machine that is the human body. Share with your friends and your families what you have learned. It is up to all of us living together as a community to care for our well-being, and to continue working for a healthier quality of life.

1

FOOD AND DIGESTION

ow long has it been since you last ate something? If you had your last meal or snack several hours ago, you are probably a little hungry. If you are like most people, the longer you go without eating, the more uncomfortable you become. If too much time passes, you may begin to have the stomach contractions that cause hunger pangs. You may even become grouchy and irritable, and your head may begin to ache—signals, sent by your body, that its trillions of cells need nourishment in order to stay active and in good repair.

The importance of food has been acknowledged by every civilization throughout history. Even in parts of the world where food is consistently scarce, ceremonial gatherings have always centered around food. In more affluent cultures, holidays and social events are traditionally associated with special foods and elaborate feasts. In modern society, food figures integrally in almost every social and leisure activity.

For all our interest in and involvement with food, few people understand its real importance to the body. What actually happens to the 100,000 pounds of food that the average American consumes in a lifetime? How do the foods we ingest during a meal find their way to body cells? How are they used by the body? Why are some foods better for us than others? How much food is enough? How much is too little? Why will the body die if it is deprived of food?

Actually, food, as such, is not of value to the body. The foods we eat act as convenient and tasty packaging for special chemicals called nutrients. Small amounts of nutrients are needed every single day by every

A Thanksgiving dinner. Food plays a central role in holiday celebrations and social events in all parts of the world.

The digestive process breaks down the nutrients found in a glass of milk into simple molecules that are essential to every bodily function.

cell in the body. The foods we eat contain, within chemical compounds, molecules of carbohydrates, proteins, fats, vitamins, minerals, and water. Many people are surprised to learn that water is a nutrient. In fact, water is so important to the body that it will die sooner from a shortage of water than from a deprivation of any other nutrient.

Nutrients not only supply the body's cells with enough energy to carry on their life processes but also serve as the raw materials for building, repairing, and controlling our body systems. In order to accomplish these jobs, nutrients must break away from their large compounds and change their chemical forms, becoming simple molecules that are small enough to pass through the membranes that cover a cell. A glass of milk, for example, is a food package containing sugar, fat, calcium, vitamin D, protein, and water. When milk is taken into the body, it goes through a series of physical and chemical changes, each of which helps the nutrients to separate from the milk and become simpler molecules. Once all the changes have occurred, the nutrients can pass into the body cells and begin their jobs. The process in the body that makes these changes possible is called digestion.

The digestive system is made up of those organs in the body that work together to change foods into nutrients. Most of these organs make up the alimentary canal, a tube that is approximately 30 feet long and has many twists and turns. It begins at the mouth and includes the esophagus, the stomach, and the small and large intestines. In addition, the liver and the pancreas, two organs located outside the alimentary canal, also help in the process of digestion.

Together, these organs of the digestive system perform a remarkable task. They mechanically chop, mash, churn, and mix foods into a soupy paste. During digestion, complex chemical changes take place. Chemical changes always happen more quickly and precisely when molecules themselves move quickly, a condition stimulated by high temperature. Yet the temperature of the digestive system rarely tops 100°F. Even so, the chemical reactions that occur within the body are faster and more accurate than those achieved by chemists working in the best laboratories at much higher temperatures.

This activity is only one of the mysteries of the digestive system. Another concerns the various functions performed by the digestive organs. Consider, for example, the stomach, which—during digestion—releases hydrochloric acid. This acid is so strong that it is capable of burning a hole through a thick carpet. Yet hydrochloric acid does not burn a hole in the walls of the stomach. It is equally amazing that the glands of living tissues can produce this corrosive acid in the first place.

And there are other mysteries as well. Why is it, for instance, that the stomach does not digest itself? This organ is able to break down tripe, the stomach lining of a cow, yet it does not cannibalize its own lining. Another mystery involves the way in which digestion acts on food proteins. Other body systems normally fight off and reject foreign proteins. Why is it that the digestive system selectively absorbs, changes, and uses proteins for the body's benefit?

Digestion, in other words, is a complicated process. An average meal takes anywhere from 15 hours to 2 days to pass through the entire alimentary canal. It is also a dependent process, one entirely reliant upon the materials that are ingested. The system must respond to the five or six smaller meals—including snacks—that many people consume each day. If no food is taken in, no normal digestion takes place. But the digestive system does not allow the body cells to die easily. In cases of severe starvation, where no energy nutrients are available and all stored nutrients have been used up, the system will attempt to digest other body tissues to keep the body alive.

Efficient digestion is an important factor in maintaining a healthy body. Because the conditions under which digestion takes place often determine whether or not food is properly digested, it would seem that most people, because they can control these conditions, can also maintain a well-nourished body. But proper nourishment is easier to understand than to achieve.

Many facets of our behavior and habits affect how we digest food. Millions of people regularly eat on the run, skip meals, and consume fast foods. Millions overeat, binge on junk food, or blindly embark on fashionable but harmful diets. The digestive system is equipped to process or absorb every known nutrient. It can store only a few nutrients for later use, however, and it cannot compensate for deficient quantities of nutrients.

It follows, then, that understanding digestion may be a valuable step toward developing a healthier body. You may find healthier ways of

No one with poor eating habits can maintain a healthy body. Junk food does not provide the body with sufficient nutrients, and the digestive system cannot compensate for this deficiency.

eating as you become more familiar with the nutrients the body needs and with the system that prepares these vital nutrients for use in the cells. Becoming better acquainted with the digestive system may help you to develop respect for the life-sustaining functions that so many people unwisely take for granted. Understanding the digestive system may also help you to take better care of the remarkable organs that work within it, and, in turn, to live with a better-nourished and healthier body.

2

A HISTORY
OF DIGESTION

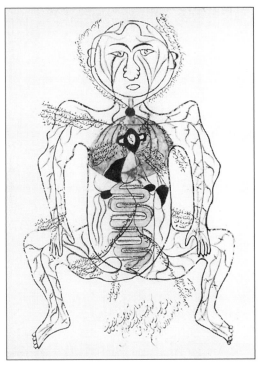

A 15th-century anatomical drawing.

Most food must undergo a series of physical and chemical changes before it can be used by the body's cells and tissues. Through the process of digestion, nature has provided living things with a way of changing food into substances that are necessary to sustain life.

To understand this more clearly, consider the automobile, a machine that, like the body, needs fuel in order to operate. The raw material from which automobile fuel is made is extracted from underground in the form of crude oil. We cannot fill a gas tank with this oil, however, until it has been changed into gasoline by a chemical process.

Similarly, food must be transformed into efficient fuel. One way of doing this was discovered thousands of years ago by our Neanderthal ancestors, who stumbled upon cooking over an open flame as a means of preparing food for consumption. These ancient people unwittingly found a way to break down fibers in meat and cellulose in plants, making these staples of their diet easier to eat and digest.

Every developing culture has continued to understand that food must be prepared for eating and must be chewed and moistened as it passes from the mouth into the stomach. The ancient Greeks were aware that food reaches the stomach through a narrow tube that they named the *esophagus,* after a word that means "to carry away what is eaten." But for many centuries, no one understood the changes that take place once food reaches the stomach. Indeed, physicians believed that food simply stayed in the stomach and decayed there. It was not until the early 1700s that the first hint of the real process of digestion was discovered.

At that time, René de Réaumur, a French scientist, performed unprecedented experiments on his pet bird. The bird was a kite, a species that has the protective ability to regurgitate, or vomit up, anything it cannot digest. Réaumur lowered tiny pieces of sponge into the bird's stomach. The kite did not regurgitate the sponges, but instead began to digest them. When Réaumur pulled up the sponges, he found they had absorbed very powerful juices. Réaumur tested the juices and found they could dissolve bits of meat into liquid.

This discovery convinced Réaumur and other scientists that the stomach secretes, or gives off, juices that help change certain foods. This was the first time the scientific world considered the stomach to be a vital digestive organ. But Réaumur's experiments, important as they were, did not add much to our knowledge about the process that occurs in the human stomach. It took another century and a most unlikely accident before the medical world made its first true observations of the workings of the human digestive system.

On June 6, 1822 in Fort Michilimackinac, Michigan, Alexis St. Martin, an 18-year-old French Canadian, accidentally shot himself with a musket that fired lead and wadding (paper material used in cartridges) into his body and left a gaping hole in his left side. One of St. Martin's ribs was partly destroyed, another was fractured, his left lung was damaged, and his stomach was pierced. Ordinarily, such wounds would have left the victim dead within a few hours. But Dr. William Beaumont, a surgeon in the United States Army who rushed to St. Martin's aid, pushed the young man's lung and stomach back into his chest and attended to the wounds as best he could. St. Martin not only survived his terrible injury but was on the road to good health after only a few weeks.

The opening in St. Martin's stomach wall did not close, however. He was left with a small tunnel that led directly through skin and muscle into his stomach. Even when he was fully recovered and eager to eat, the food leaked out of the open wound. Beaumont fed his patient through the anus, and did whatever he could to close the stomach opening, which was two and a half inches in circumference and situated about two inches below the left nipple. St. Martin, who would not permit the doctor to operate, found he could eat and drink if bandages were plugged into the opening in his stomach. As long as the bandages remained in place, St. Martin digested his food as before, and the opening did not harm any of his other organs.

An illustration of Dr. William Beaumont (right) and Alexis St. Martin. After an accident left a hole in St. Martin's stomach in 1822, Dr. Beaumont observed the workings of his patient's digestive system.

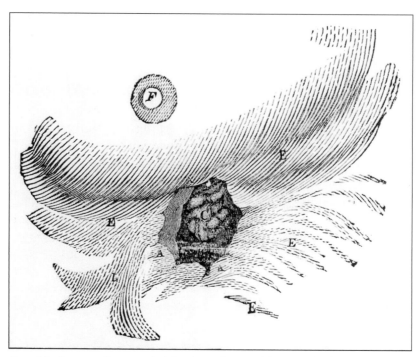

One of Dr. Beaumont's anatomical drawings of St. Martin's stomach. The doctor's observations enabled him to identify such essential components of digestion as hydrochloric acid and pepsin.

After two years of tending his patient, Dr. Beaumont realized that the unique fistula, or false opening, in the stomach of his patient could be used as a kind of observation window. Dr. Beaumont offered St. Martin free room and board in exchange for his participation in some painless experiments that ultimately made medical history. Beaumont had no laboratory, no skilled assistants, and no specialized knowledge of digestion. Nonetheless, the experiments he devised broke ground for all the subsequent research on digestion.

Beaumont weighed small amounts of food, tied them to silk thread, and lowered them through the hole into St. Martin's stomach. He removed the food every hour, observed how it had changed while in the stomach, and replaced it. By withdrawing the food when it was partly digested, Beaumont was able to confirm that the stomach secretes strong digestive juices. He also removed some of the juices and, after testing them, identified hydrochloric acid as a gastric, or stomach, juice.

At the same time, Beaumont found another juice, later identified as the enzyme pepsin. He also observed that the stomach contracted and remained empty when no food was eaten for a time and that it became flushed with blood when St. Martin was angry.

St. Martin was not an ideal subject for study. He was often moody and uncooperative. Beaumont had to follow him, at the doctor's own expense, from one place to another to keep his experiments going. Sometimes St. Martin would simply leave and not return for a period of time. Once, he disappeared for four years, and returned as a subject only after Beaumont tracked him down. But in spite of these difficulties, Dr. Beaumont's experiments continued over a period of eight years. During all this time, St. Martin remained in excellent health. He worked at strenuous jobs and enjoyed a normal and healthy appetite. He was able to eat foods that needed no special softening or preparation, and he outlived Beaumont by 27 years, dying at the age of 76. As a result of his work with Alexis St. Martin, Beaumont published his conclusions in an 1833 article, "Experiments and Observations on Gastric Juice and the Physiology of Digestion." (The article was reprinted by Dover Publications in 1959.)

All told, Beaumont drew from his experiments some 50 "inferences," as he called them, about digestion. In addition to identifying hydrochloric acid and another gastric juice in the stomach, Beaumont noted that no matter what food St. Martin ingested the stomach acted in the same manner. The doctor also learned that bulk was as important as nutrition in eating properly. Beaumont discovered further that alcohol—"stimulating condiments," in his words—harmed the stomach. These observations about the stomach and about the way in which food passes through the body were the most significant contributions that had yet been made to the study of digestion.

In 1833, the same year that William Beaumont published the results of his experiments, two French chemists, Anselme Payen and Jean Peroz, made another discovery about digestion when they found the enzyme diastase, a substance in the human body that helps change starch into sugar. Later, dozens more enzymes would be identified as participants in the digestive process. But another 100 years passed before anyone in the medical world had the opportunity to work directly with human digestion again.

In 1895, a nine-year-old boy, known only as Tom in the annals of medical history, swallowed what he thought was beer but what turned out to be steaming-hot clam chowder. The boiling soup burned Tom's

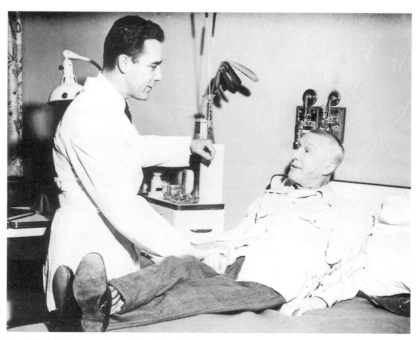

Tom (right) became the subject of study for Drs. Stewart Wolf and Harold Wolff, who were intrigued by the possible effects of emotions on the human stomach.

esophagus and closed it off from his stomach. The boy was rushed to a hospital, but surgeons could not unblock his esophagus. Instead, they performed a gastrostomy, an operation in which an artificial channel to the stomach is created, which would bypass the esophagus and still allow Tom to feed himself. During the surgery, however, something went wrong, and the surgeon had to finish the operation without closing Tom's stomach. As a result, Tom recovered but was left with a one-and-a-half-inch opening into his stomach.

Somehow, Tom learned to digest his food in a most peculiar way. He would chew it up and spit it into a funnel attached to a rubber tube that led into his stomach. Tom ate twice a day and had to wait five hours between each meal until his stomach was empty. If he failed to do this, the food would spill over. Despite this awkward procedure, Tom led a fairly normal life.

Tom was able to keep his stomach opening a secret from most people, even doctors, for more than 40 years. Problems arose in 1939, when he got a job as a ditchdigger. The steady movement of his pick against the bandage over his fistula caused it to bleed.

Tom lost a great deal of blood and was rushed to a hospital, where he came to the attention of Dr. Stewart Wolf and Dr. Harold Wolff. The 2 doctors realized that the 53-year-old patient provided the same opportunity for study that Alexis St. Martin had afforded William Beaumont more than a century earlier.

Unlike Beaumont, Drs. Wolf and Wolff were especially interested in the damage wrought on the stomach by long-term emotional upsets. It took the physicians a few months to persuade Tom to help them in their research. The results justified the wait. Experiments showed that Tom's emotions could indeed trigger physical reactions in his stomach. For example, when he was aggressive or resentful, his stomach reacted as if it were getting ready for a meal: It secreted digestive juices, and the lining of the stomach filled with blood. When Tom was sad or afraid, depressed or withdrawn, his stomach did not react: No juices appeared, and the stomach lining remained pink and bloodless. The experiments also showed that a strong emotional reaction can dominate appetite—some people will eat more when they are upset, for example, whereas others will lose their desire to eat. In addition, the doctors learned that emotional reactions can speed up the digestive process and cause the stomach to produce too much acid, which is carried up to the esophagus or down to the small intestine. Here, there is no protective lining to prevent the patient from developing ailments ranging from minor heartburn to serious ulcers.

The connection between ulcers and stomach acids was known as far back as the 7th century A.D., when Paul of Aegina, a Byzantine physician, wrote, "When there is an ulcer in the stomach or bowels, the patient must abstain from all acid food or drink." This remarkable insight into the workings of the stomach was confirmed by Drs. Wolf and Wolff as they peered through Tom's "peephole."

DISCOVERING VITAMINS

At the same time that some scientists were adding to our knowledge of digestion, others began to explore foods and the substances in them that are essential to growth and good health. The idea that foods contain vital substances was not a 20th-century discovery, however. The ancient Greek physician Hippocrates (c. 460–377 B.C.)—the "father of modern medicine"—recommended that people eat liver (now known

In the 7th century, Byzantine scientist Paul of Aegina observed the connection between ulcers and stomach acids.

to be rich in vitamin A) to cure night blindness, a condition in which the eyes adjust slowly to changes in light. And in the 16th century, Indians living in the Canadian province now known as Quebec concocted a leafy brew that helped cure French explorers plagued with scurvy, a disease characterized by spongy gums, loose teeth, and bleeding of the skin and mucous membranes. The Indians' remedy undoubtedly contained vitamin C, which is still acknowledged as the vital ingredient in combating scurvy. In the 18th century, oil taken from cod and related fish became a standard cure-all in England. Cod-liver oil is rich in vitamins A and D. During the 19th century, the Japanese fed barley to sailors afflicted with beriberi, a condition in which the feet and legs often become swollen and paralyzed.

Beriberi was also rampant among prisoners in the East Indies in the late 19th century. In 1897, Dr. Christiaan Eijkman, a Dutch physician and medical officer, observed that chickens in the prison where he was stationed showed symptoms of beriberi. Dr. Eijkman realized that the chickens ate the same rice diet as the prisoners, and so he conducted some experiments. He found that when the fowl consumed polished

The ancient Greek physician Hippocrates shrewdly recommended that people eat liver, a food now known to be rich in vitamin A, to cure night blindness.

rice—rice whose outer coating had been discarded—they did not suffer beriberi. Dr. Eijkman concluded that beriberi must be caused by some poisonous substance in rice that could be destroyed by polishing. This was close to the mark but not quite accurate. In fact, rice polishing did not rid the food of a poisonous substance but, rather, polished rice contained a substance the chickens needed. In 1910, an American chemist, Robert R. Williams, isolated the special substance: vitamin B_1, or thiamine.

The period from 1910 to 1913 was critical to the development of a theory of vitamin supplements. Essential chemicals were being isolated, but the idea that deficiency diseases were not caused by germs caught on only very slowly. The germ theory itself was only half a century old, and it still held attraction for physicians and researchers.

One of the pioneers of modern food study was Dr. Frederick Gowland Hopkins, a professor of physiology at England's Cambridge University. In the early years of the 20th century, Dr. Hopkins experimented with the diets of white rats. He discovered that fats, proteins, and carbohydrates alone are not enough to sustain life. The body

Polish scientist Casimir Funk first called the accessory food factors required by the body vitamins (from the Latin vita, *for life), a word that has since passed into common usage.*

required other "accessory food factors," as he called them, to remain alive and well. In 1912, Casimir Funk, a Polish scientist working in England, gave these food factors a more memorable name, vitamins (derived from *vita,* Latin for "life").

Dr. Hopkins, who was knighted in 1925 and received the Nobel Prize in physiology in 1929, was not alone in the search for important substances in food. In 1913, an American scientist, Dr. E. V. McCollum, conducted experiments on the diets of white mice at the University of Wisconsin. He and Dr. Lafayette Mendel of Yale University found that butterfat improved a serious infection in the rats' eyes. They isolated a special substance in butterfat, and it became the first individual vitamin to be named—vitamin A. Since that time, scientists have discovered that even a moderate lack of vitamin A causes night blindness.

As other individual vitamins were isolated and identified, they always received letter names. Ascorbic acid, the substance that prevents scurvy, was dubbed vitamin C. In 1922, Dr. E. V. McCollum, who had earlier identified vitamin A, was working at Johns Hopkins University. He and the members of his research team studied the contents of cod-liver oil and discovered vitamin D. This substance does not appear in large amounts in ordinary foods, but a more common substance, ergosterol, can be changed to vitamin D by exposure to ultraviolet light.

Another vitamin-deficiency disease is pellagra, which occurs mainly in people whose diets are lacking in fresh meat and milk. The disease appeared as early as 1735 and in 1 year, 1930, took 7,000 lives in the United States. Dr. Joseph Goldberger of the United States Public Health Service noted that pellagra did not infect attending doctors and nurses, and he departed from conventional wisdom by deciding it was not caused by a germ. He changed the diets of children at a Missouri orphanage and within a year entirely eliminated pellagra there. Dr. Goldberger then experimented with volunteer subjects at the Rankin Prison

In 1922 Dr. E. V. McCollum and his research team identified the healing contents of cod-liver oil as vitamin D.

Farm in Georgia, and caused pellagra in seven of 11 men who had been given diets of corn meal, white bread, flour, potatoes, salt pork, and syrup. The vitamin that was missing from the diets of these prisoners, a member of the vitamin B family, was given the name niacin. The search for a cure for pellagra led to the identification of another B vitamin, called B_2, or riboflavin. This nutrient was originally called vitamin G by the German chemist who discovered it in 1932. Much of the German research involving food factors was the result of the food shortages created by World War I. In 1921, three years after the end of that war, three vitamins had been identified. Today, some 40 vitamins are known, and at least 12 of them are essential to good nutrition.

The groundwork for understanding the operation of the digestive system was laid by Dr. William Beaumont and all the research pioneers who followed. There is a great deal left to learn, however. Modern technology has helped expand our knowledge of this complex process. Scientists have learned much, for example, by observing how human digestion occurs in astronauts in gravity-free space capsules. And on a less exalted plane, ordinary people also are taking more interest in proper eating habits. The next chapter discusses the nutrients our body needs and the foods that contain them.

3

UNDERSTANDING NUTRIENTS

N utrients, the substances that keep us alive, appear in a wide variety of foods that the human digestive system efficiently breaks down, changing their complex chemical compounds into simple, usable molecules. Nonetheless, there is a limit to what humans can eat and digest. Indeed, the human digestive system cannot cope with most of the plants, trees, and mosses consumed by more than half the world's animals. Many foods that keep other creatures alive do humans no good at all. Other substances either make humans seriously ill or kill them.

To stay alive and well, the human body requires some 30 to 40 special chemical compounds, in addition to the 6 essential nutrients. These substances, which are found in different types of food, all contribute to the well-being of the human body.

CARBOHYDRATES

In order to perform activities such as breathing, running, and working, the body needs energy in all its cells. It derives this energy from the foods we eat. In fact, most of the food we eat is used by the body to produce energy. The most important source of day-to-day energy for most people comes from nutrients known as carbohydrates.

There are two main types of carbohydrates: sugars and starches. Chemically, they are composed of carbon, hydrogen and oxygen. Normally, carbohydrates contain a ratio of two hydrogen atoms to one oxygen atom, and the general formula for any carbohydrate (or hydrated carbon) is written as $C_x(H_2O)Y_5$. Carbohydrates range from simple

Participants in a New York City Marathon. To perform any activity—from running a race to simply sitting and thinking—the body requires the energy furnished by carbohydrates, proteins, and fats.

sugars, which contain a few carbon atoms, to complex compounds (polysaccharides), large groups of simple sugars joined together to form giant units, such as starch.

Carbohydrates are not as rich in energy as are fats, another nutrient, but the energy in carbohydrates is easier for the body to use. The body steadily employs carbohydrates, storing only limited quantities that it changes into glycogen. This substance remains in the liver and muscles as a source of reserve energy. Excess carbohydrates that are not stored as glycogen are changed to fat and stored in special body tissues.

Sugars, which come in many different forms, are called simple carbohydrates. They are found in milk, fruits, nuts and vegetables. Sugar is also added as a sweetener to candies, cakes, puddings, and other desserts. In the terminology of chemistry, sugars are easily identified by the ending -ose. Table sugar is known as sucrose; many fruits contain a sugar called fructose. Maltose is a sugar found in barley, and lactose is a milk sugar. Whatever form sugar is in originally, the body breaks it down into glucose, a very simple molecule. Many nutritionists believe that the average person annually ingests almost five times as much sugar as the body needs. A study entitled "Dietary Sugar Disease" by Dr. Aaron M. Cohen of Hebrew University Hadassah Medical College, published by The United States Senate Select Committee on Nutrition and Human Needs, has shown a distinct relation between high sugar intake and arterial and heart disease.

Starches are complex carbohydrates found in breads, cereals, potatoes, rice, and pasta (such as spaghetti and macaroni). As it does with sugars, the body transforms all starches into glucose. Complex carbohydrates are a better source of sustained energy than are sugars. Marathon runners eat a diet rich in starches for several days before a long run because the reserves of glycogen their body stores keep their energy going over a long period of strenuous activity.

Carbohydrates are essential for survival. Areas of the world where food products contain low supplies of carbohydrates often suffer high incidences of starvation. This could be avoided if cellulose, a major carbohydrate found in all plants, could be processed by the human digestive system. Cellulose appears in all forms of vegetation and can be digested by herbivores, animals such as cows and sheep that graze on grasses. Unfortunately, cellulose does not affect the human body; it is expelled completely with human waste materials.

Malnourished Ethiopian children. In areas of the world where the food supply contains low quantities of carbohydrates there is often an extremely high incidence of starvation.

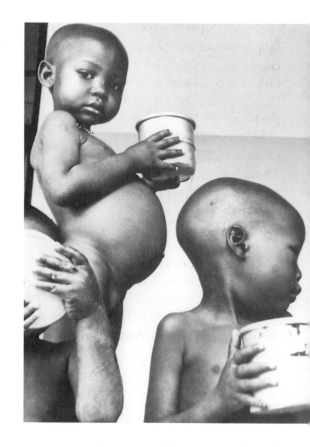

FATS

Milk products, egg whites, nuts, meats, and oils supply the body with essential nutrients called fats. They are an important substance for every cell and are used as part of many cell activities. Fats carry some vitamins to cells that need them and serve to cushion internal organs. They also are an important store of body energy.

A typical fat molecule is a chain of carbon atoms tied to a series of hydrogen atoms. There is nothing more than an occasional oxygen atom at the end of the chain, which means no water (H_2O) is locked up in a fat molecule. Because water is not a fuel but simply dead weight, fats release a higher proportion of energy than do water-laden carbohydrates. Fats that take a liquid form at room temperature are called oils. However, there is no chemical difference between fats and oils. Olive oil, for instance, is simply a liquid form of olive fat.

Fats taken into the body as food must be altered by the digestive system. They are emulsified, or broken into smaller globules, by bile, a chemical produced by the liver and stored in the gallbladder. When the body has completely digested fat, the substance becomes a fatty acid. Once digested fats assume these forms, they can be used by the cells in the body.

Some fat is not immediately changed for use but stored in the liver or under the skin—as fat cells used as an insulator—for future use. About half the body's stored fat, however, attaches to the mesentery, a membrane that supports the small intestine. More fat is also stored around the kidneys.

The body demands a small amount of fat, but an excess of the substance is unhealthy. In fact, the intake of certain fats has been linked to serious heart disease. These fats—saturated animal fats—contain cholesterol, a substance that, although produced within the body itself, is dangerous if it exists in excess. Healthier fats—called unsaturated because their carbon atoms are not saturated with their full potential of surrounding hydrogen atoms— are contained in margarine and in vegetable oils.

PROTEINS

About 18% of human body weight consists of protein molecules. Proteins are nutrients needed by every cell for growth and repair. They are the most complex compounds in the body, which can use them only after it has broken them down through digestion into their basic element: amino acids.

Like carbohydrates and fats, proteins consist of carbon, hydrogen, and oxygen. In addition, each protein molecule contains nitrogen, an essential element that is excreted with urine when body proteins become damaged. Proteins are also a major source of sulfur, a necessary mineral.

What makes proteins vital, however, is their amino acids. The process of digestion creates increasingly simpler amino acids, which the body then uses to build molecules such as hemoglobin, the protein compound in red blood cells that carries oxygen. Many amino acids become the raw materials for building new tissues, such as skin. They are also used to repair damaged and aging cells. Proteins, though especially important while the body is growing, figure crucially in adult diets as well. Although protein is primarily a building nutrient, it is also an emergency source of energy for the body. Carbohydrates and fats are the body's main energy fuels. In emergencies, however, the body can turn proteins into sugar and use them to produce needed energy.

Meat, fish, milk, eggs, whole grains, lentils, and beans are good sources of protein. There is a shortage of protein on earth, however, and this lack is the greatest single cause of malnutrition, a condition resulting from a diet poor in quality, not quantity. People who consume a great deal of food but not the right foods can suffer from malnutrition.

MINERALS

Carbohydrates, fats, and proteins contain carbon, hydrogen, oxygen, nitrogen, and sulfur—elements essential to the human body. They are not all the body requires, however. It also must replenish its constantly diminishing supply of minerals. During the digestive process minerals do not change chemically but are absorbed into the body for use. Only a small quantity of minerals is needed by the body, but their absence can prove damaging. Iodine, for example, is essential to the human diet, but the body needs only a few millionths of an ounce of this nutrient per day.

Calcium builds strong bones and teeth. It helps blood to clot and muscles to contract properly. Many foods, including milk, egg yolk, cereals, and some vegetables, contain calcium, but most of the mineral passes out of the body with solid wastes.

Phosphorus is also needed for strong bones and teeth, and it is part of the fat content of body cells. Good sources of this mineral include fish, milk, cheese, eggs, vegetables, and cereals.

Iron is an important part of the blood's hemoglobin. This mineral is found in body chemicals called enzymes and in the liver. Foods that contain iron include liver, kidney, eggs, vegetables, and cereals. Because milk contains so little iron, babies who are fed only milk for more than six months may suffer from an iron deficiency.

Iodine helps the thyroid gland, important because it controls physical growth, to function properly. The thyroid contains more than half the iodine in the body. In most parts of the world, water and vegetables provide people with the tiny amount of iodine they need each day.

Sodium is found in the bones and in the body fluids. Very little sodium is actually inside the cells and very little needs to be added. More than enough enters the body in an average diet. For this reason, adding sodium, which is most commonly available in the form of table salt (sodium chloride), may be harmful. Unfortunately, many people take in more salt than the body needs.

Potassium is a mineral found largely within the cells and is the essential cation, or ion, of muscle and other cells. Low potassium levels can cause severe muscle problems, such as paralysis or heart failure. Bananas and avocados are good sources of potassium.

Magnesium is a mineral essential to nutrition, for it is required for the activity of digestive enzymes. A lack of magnesium can cause irritability of the nervous system, depression, tremors, convulsions, and psychotic behavior.

Chlorine plays an important role in balancing the amount of water that enters and leaves body cells. It also aids digestion, activates enzymes, and is essential to normal gastric secretion.

Other body minerals include the essential trace minerals, copper, cobalt, zinc, manganese, and molybdenum. These five minerals weigh less than a gram combined. They play essential roles in the formation of important body enzymes, and therefore must be present in the body.

Bananas are a good source of potassium, a mineral that is the essential ion found in muscles and cells.

VITAMINS

Each vitamin differs from every other, yet all consist of a combination of chemicals that the body requires. The most important vitamins include the following:

Vitamin A (retinol) is found in liver, fish, dairy products, eggs, carrots, green vegetables, and margarine. Deficiency of this vitamin causes night blindness, dry and inflamed eyes, lack of resistance to infection, and bad skin. Vitamin A also plays a role in regulating cell growth. It is fat soluble (it dissolves in and is carried by fat cells) and can be stored within the body. An excess of this vitamin, however, can cause such symptoms as painful swellings and loss of hair.

Vitamin B$_1$ (thiamine) is found in carbohydrate-rich foods such as bread, flour, meat, and milk. A low supply of this vitamin can cause beriberi (see Chapter 2). This vitamin is essential to the body's digestive process, growth, and muscle tone. It helps carbohydrates release energy.

Vitamin B$_2$ (riboflavin) is found in milk, liver, eggs, and green vegetables. It is necessary for converting food to energy.

Vitamin B$_6$ (pyridoxine) is found in liver, yeast, cereals, bread, milk products, and eggs. It is involved in the rebuilding of protein molecules. Vitamin B$_6$ may also help the blood to clot.

Vitamin B$_{12}$ (cyanocobalamin) is found in dairy and animal products. Vitamin B$_{12}$ is also made by bacteria in the intestinal tract. It is needed by cells that divide very rapidly, such as those in the bone marrow that form blood. Vitamin B$_{12}$ also contributes to a healthy nervous system and to proper growth.

Biotin is found in egg yolk, liver, kidney, and yeast. Like vitamin B$_{12}$, it can be made by intestinal bacteria. It is part of several enzyme systems in the body, and helps in cell growth and in the production of fatty acids.

Folic Acid is found in most leafy vegetables, bread, oranges, and bananas. It is needed by cells such as those in bone marrow and, if taken early in pregnancy, may help prevent some birth defects.

Nicotinic Acid (niacin) is found in lean meats, enriched cereals and bread, eggs, and milk products. It helps in the digestive process that changes food into energy. It also helps the body to maintain a healthy nervous system, a good appetite, and healthy skin. A deficiency of this vitamin can cause the skin disease pellagra.

Pantothenic Acid is found in nearly all foods. The body requires it for growth, for the production of antibodies to fight infections, and for the chemical breakdown of fats and carbohydrates.

Vitamin C crystals. This substance, which is found in fresh fruits and green vegetables, not only helps maintain healthy teeth and gums but may also play a part in fighting infection.

Vitamin C (ascorbic acid) is found in fresh fruits—especially citrus fruits—and in green vegetables, potatoes, and tomatoes. It is important for healthy teeth, gums, and bones. Vitamin C may play a part in fighting infection and breaking down cholesterol. A lack of vitamin C may result in scurvy.

Vitamin D (calciferol) is not strictly a vitamin because the body can produce it. In fact, sunlight helps the body manufacture vitamin D. It is, rather, a hormone—a chemical manufactured in the body. Outside the body, vitamin D is found in cod-liver oil, egg yolk, salmon, tuna, butter, and in specially fortified milk. The body requires vitamin D in order to maintain proper levels of calcium and phosphorus in the blood and to transport calcium to and from the bones. Vitamin D is another fat-soluble substance. Too much of it may cause hypercalcemia, a disorder that can lead to mental retardation in babies.

Vitamin E (tocopherol) is found in vegetable oils, wheat germ, eggs, nuts, fruits, and green vegetables. Vitamin E helps keep the membranes of red blood cells healthy. It has also been credited with preventing blindness in premature babies. The benefits of vitamin E, a fat-soluble vitamin, are still being studied.

Vitamin K (phylloquinone) is found in green vegetables, oatmeal, and liver. It is needed for normal clotting of the blood. There are two forms of this vitamin, K_1 and K_2. The latter is produced by bacteria in the intestines. Babies that are born with an inadequate supply of vitamin K may suffer a hemorrhagic (severe bleeding) disease. They need extra vitamin K for about three days, or until their own body begins to manufacture the vitamin.

WATER

Water, the most abundant chemical in the human body, is also its most essential nutrient; the body will die more quickly from a deprivation of water than from a lack of any other substance.

All other nutrients enter the cell only after they have dissolved in water, which is able to dissolve most materials. Water is a stable substance; it carries many chemicals without itself changing. It is also an efficient cooling agent and vaporizes easily.

The body constantly loses and replenishes its water supply— at an average rate of about five pints of water per day. Water is lost in urine and in solid waste. It is lost as perspiration and as vapor through the lungs. In turn, about half of the food we eat is water. Therefore, we can take in about three-fifths of a pint of water at each meal without drinking any extra water at all. Another three-fourths of a pint of water is created by the body as the waste materials of energy production. The remaining three and a half pints of water lost daily should be replenished by drinking the liquid. Indeed, everyone should drink at least one quart of water each day.

The body requires a supply of all its essential nutrients every single day. In order to remain healthy, the body must maintain a diet that includes a balanced quantity of necessary carbohydrates, fats, proteins, minerals, vitamins, and water. Once armed with raw materials, the digestive system takes over—through a process described in the next chapter.

4

THE PROCESS
OF DIGESTION

A photomicrograph of the trachea lining.

hink about the last meal you ate. In all probability, the food you swallowed contained many of the nutrients your body needs. But in order to be of use to your cells, these nutrients must undergo some changes over a period of several hours. The process whereby these foods change into nutrients is chemical, and results from the joint effort of those organs that make up the digestive system.

A CHEMICAL PROCESS

The goal of the digestive process is to change useful chemicals in foods into molecules that can pass through the small intestine and be processed in the blood. Some nutrients, such as minerals and vitamins, need to be changed only physically. As they dissolve in water, they are reduced into molecules that enter the digestive system. A small number of vitamins are fat soluble.

The task of facilitating the chemical reactions that change large, complex molecules into simple, usable ones is much more complicated. The nutrients that undergo these changes are carbohydrates (sugars and starches), proteins, and fats.

To understand this more clearly, consider that table sugar (sucrose) is chemically known as a disaccharide, or double sugar. A disaccharide forms when 2 simple sugars combine into 45 bonded atoms—12 carbon atoms, 22 hydrogen atoms, and 11 oxygen atoms. The chemical formula for a double sugar is $C_{12}H_{22}O_{11}$. During digestion, each large molecule of sugar must be changed into a monosaccharide, or simple sugar, such as glucose (dextrose).

A large molecule can split into smaller molecules through hydrolysis, a process whereby a molecule of glucose, for example, combines with a water molecule (H_2O). A glucose molecule has 6 carbon atoms, 12 hydrogen atoms, and 6 oxygen atoms ($C_6H_{12}O_6$). Notice that two glucose molecules have one more water molecule than one molecule of a double sugar. The glucose molecule, which contains a total of 24 atoms, is less complex than a molecule of sucrose.

Most nutrients enter the body as parts of other compounds. Sugar, for instance, might be baked into a pie or consumed naturally in milk. Extremely complex chains of protein form integral parts of eggs, meats, and cheeses. Similarly, fats are derived from animal and vegetable sources. All these nutrients must undergo digestive processes that separate the nutrients from their host foods and then break them down into end products, or simple forms. One cannot understand the activities of digestion without examining how and where these changes occur.

THE MOUTH

Human digestion begins in the mouth, which is located at the beginning of the alimentary canal, or food tube, through which all food must pass as it is processed by the digestive system. This tube, which is

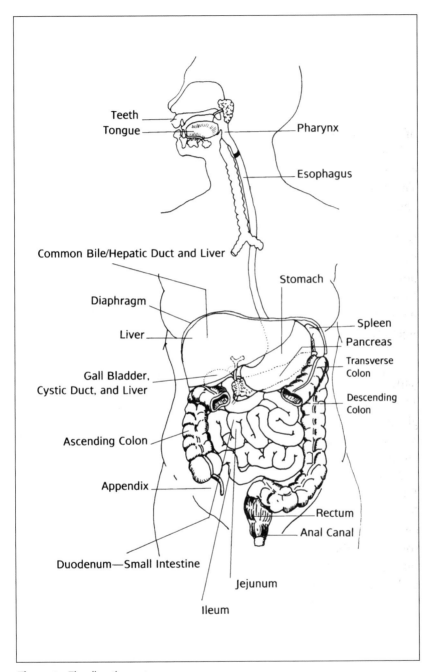

Figure 1: The digestive system.

approximately 30 feet long, is folded over and over in the abdomen like a pile of rope. It is made up of the mouth, the esophagus, the stomach, and the small and large intestines. Assisting the organs of the alimentary canal are the liver, the body's largest gland, and the pancreas, a smaller gland. Each of these organs plays a distinct part in breaking down food.

The process of digestion begins even before anything is eaten, when we see and smell appetizing food. Three sets of salivary glands—located under the jaw (submandibular gland), under the tongue (sublingual gland), and next to the ear (parotid gland)— whet our urge to consume food by releasing saliva, the liquid that makes the mouth water at the mere sight of a juicy steak or at the inviting aroma of fresh pizza. It pours continually into the mouth, bathing the teeth and moistening the mouth and throat. Saliva also helps moisten food so that it slips more easily down the throat.

The sight and smell of food, or the presence of food in the mouth, stimulate the salivary glands to secrete special enzymes, which in turn activate the first chemical change that takes place during digestion. These enzymes also initiate the chemical breakdown of starch molecules that enter the mouth.

Like the rest of the alimentary canal, the mouth contains many mucous glands in its lining. Mucus, the substance secreted by these glands, lubricates the food and helps us swallow. Once the food is moistened, the tongue pushes it against the teeth. The four sets of upper and lower incisors at the front of the mouth act as knives to slice up food. The four pointed canine teeth— two upper and two lower— which are situated on either side of the incisors, pierce and tear. The premolars and molars have broad, bumpy surfaces for grinding. All this activity is started by the jaw muscles, which grind the teeth together with great force. For their size, these muscles are probably the most powerful in the body and help the teeth chew food to a pulp in a matter of seconds.

As food is being chewed, the tongue mashes it against the palate, or roof of the mouth. The muscular tongue has an upper surface covered with papillae, small projections that aid initial digestion by causing an increase in salivary juices that makes chewing easier. When food is ready to be swallowed, the tongue pushes the lump of food, or bolus, to the back of the throat, or pharynx. The pharynx connects to two tubes, the esophagus and the trachea, or windpipe. When you swallow, the top of the trachea rises against a flap called the epiglottis. This action automatically closes the air opening that also houses the larynx, or voice box. At the same time, the back of the palate rises to block off the passage to the nose.

Try to swallow and breathe at the same time. You will find that both passages, the one from the nose and the one leading to the larynx, have been blocked. You can neither take in air nor talk while swallowing. If you swallow too quickly, or inhale a sudden gulp of air with your food, the epiglottis may not have time to close all the way. If so, you will automatically cough and thus clear out any particles of food that might have entered the trachea. Should a large piece of food lodge in the trachea, you may begin to choke. Pressure must then be applied to the diaphragm. This muscle lies just below the rib cage and above the navel

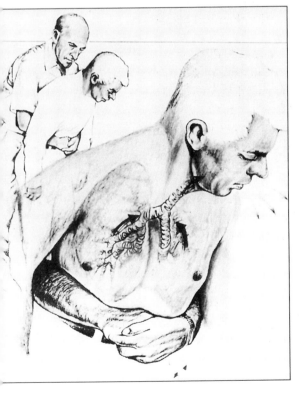

The Heimlich maneuver can save the life of a person choking on food. The maneuver involves pressing on the affected person's upper abdomen, forcing an upward surge of air that pops the food out of the mouth.

and controls air pressure in the chest cavity. Pressing on the diaphragm forces an upward surge of air that should pop the trapped food out of the mouth in a method known as the Heimlich maneuver. But normally the swallowing mechanism, by closing off the openings to the air and nasal passages, gives the food only one place to go, the next part of the alimentary canal: the esophagus.

THE ESOPHAGUS

No digestion takes place in the esophagus, but it is a vital link in the process. The esophagus is a strong, muscular tube that connects the pharynx to the stomach. It is about 10 inches long and, when empty, flattens from front to back.

In the neck, the esophagus lies between the trachea and the spine. It continues through the chest cavity, behind the heart, and connects with the stomach. The walls of the esophagus contain two layers of muscle tissue and a covering of connective tissue that produces mucus to keep the esophagus moist and smooth. The inner muscle layer of this tube is circular, and the outer layer is lengthwise. The two layers work in tandem to squeeze food down the esophagus. The ripple of muscular contractions that move the food onward is known as peristalsis.

When swallowing occurs, a muscular contraction begins at the back of the tongue and continues in a wavelike movement down the length of the esophagus. When a bolus of food enters the esophagus, rings of muscle above the bolus contract sharply, while those below it relax. This movement pushes food all the way through the digestive tract. One way to get a picture of this action is to place a ball inside a sock and then squeeze the part of the sock above the ball. This action moves the ball through the sock, much like toothpaste squeezed through a tube.

Peristalsis can carry food from the throat to the stomach in a matter of seconds. The process works no matter what position the body is in. It is even possible to eat and drink while standing on your head. Hence, astronauts in a gravity-free capsule have no difficulty eating.

At the end of the esophagus are sphincter muscles that open and close openings between different organs of the digestive system. They contract and relax to control the amount of food that can pass through. The cardiac sphincter controls the valve opening that leads to the stomach. The next stages of digestion begin as soon as food is pushed from the esophagus into its adjoining digestive organ: the stomach.

An astronaut tries to eat free-floating food. Peristalsis, a muscular contraction that pushes food through the digestive tract, makes it possible to swallow even in a gravity-free atmosphere.

THE STOMACH

Most people think the stomach is situated at the navel. Actually, it is located quite high in the body—just below and to the left of the breast-bone—and is protected by the five lowermost ribs. A baglike structure, the stomach is shaped rather like a boxing glove. Its wrist end, which connects to the small intestine, is the pyloric region. The more bulbous fingertip end, which borders on the esophagus, is the fundus.

The stomach is not absolutely vital to digestion. In fact, a number of species of vertebrates (animals with segmented spinal systems) have no stomach whatsoever. This is not surprising; after all, the vital chemi-cal changes that transform food into molecules occur after it has passed through the stomach.

Even so, the stomach has a number of useful digestive functions. It churns the food into a soupy paste, stores it for eventual passage to the small intestine, and begins the chemical breakdown of proteins in the food. If the stomach is removed, these duties are performed by the small intestine.

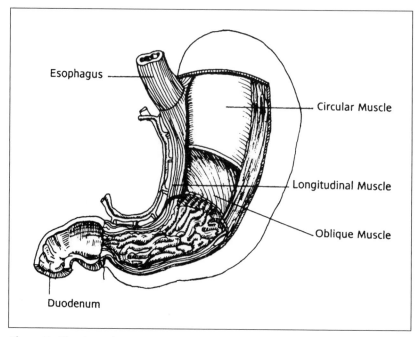

Figure 2: *The stomach.*

The stomach is a somewhat elastic organ; it can expand after a large meal to hold about two and a half pints of food. When it is empty, however, the stomach shrinks to a capacity of less than a pint. The wall of the stomach is extremely strong, and is composed of three layers that contract in different directions: lengthwise muscle, circular muscle, and oblique (slanting) muscle. These muscles enable the stomach to churn and mash food thoroughly. As the stomach fills with food, waves of peristaltic contraction spread across it every 20 seconds or so, pounding the food inside. At the same time, glands that line the stomach secrete gastric juices. Chemicals in these juices begin the breakdown of proteins in food. When food mixes with these chemicals, it forms a semifluid called chyme.

Chemicals in the Stomach

Before food enters the stomach, about 35 million glands in the stomach lining start secreting digestive juices. During a typical day, the stomach will produce a total of about four pints of gastric, or stomach, juice, including hydrochloric acid (HC1), which can burn a hole through a thick carpet. The stomach is protected from its own juices by a thick layer of mucus—another secretion of the gastric glands—that lines the stomach walls.

Hydrochloric acid performs several tasks. One is to change iron in food into a form that can later be absorbed. Another is to neutralize, or stop, the action of the enzyme amylase that was secreted in the saliva and entered the stomach from the mouth and esophagus. Amylase continues to break down starch even after the enzyme has entered the stomach. Once the acid causes the amylase to be inactive, however, no further breakdown of starch occurs, and the remaining starch must pass into the small intestine before final digestion takes place.

The most important function of hydrochloric acid is to change an inactive chemical called pepsinogen into pepsin, an active enzyme that helps break down proteins. Pepsinogen itself can be found inside the stomach glands, which helps to explain why the glands, which are made of protein, do not digest themselves. Pepsinogen cannot participate in protein breakdown until it combines with hydrochloric acid and becomes pepsin.

Pepsin begins the breakdown of proteins in the stomach by separating them into intermediate products of digestion known as peptone and proteose. Proteins are only partly hydrolyzed in the stomach. Once they reach the small intestine, peptone and proteose will finally be separated into simple amino acids, and their digestion will be complete.

Renin, another enzyme produced in the stomach, is unusual in two ways. First, it is not a digestive enzyme and thus does not change nutrients into simpler forms. Instead, renin curdles milk proteins; that is, it changes them into a solid, cheeselike state. Chemically, renin changes milk protein (caseinogen) into casein, causing it to clot.

Renin is also unusual because it operates only in the stomachs of very young babies. As an infant grows older, its stomach produces more and more acid, and soon the job of renin is completely taken over by pepsin. To this day, no one knows much about the role played by renin in adults.

Besides forming chyme and setting the breakdown of protein in motion, the stomach acts as a storage area for food during the two to six hours the organ needs to process and send on all its contents. About half an hour after we finish a meal, the chyme, a semifluid, begins to squirt toward the pyloric sphincter, which opens into the small intestine.

With each wave of peristalsis, a small quantity of chyme is pushed toward the exit valve. At first, most of it is swished back into the stomach,

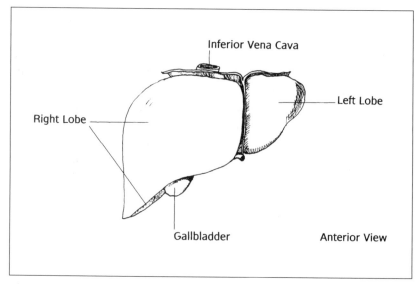

Inferior Vena Cava

Left Lobe

Right Lobe

Gallbladder

Anterior View

Figure 3: *The liver and the pancreas.*

but soon larger amounts of food move out. Foods, rich in carbohydrates leave first, followed by those rich in protein. A meal with lots of fat stays in the stomach an especially long time. Eventually, all the food in the stomach is ready for its last chemical breakdown and can be absorbed into the bloodstream.

THE LIVER AND THE PANCREAS

The most important of the digestive organs is the small intestine. It is the point from which all vital nutrients pass into the bloodstream in their final molecular forms. Because its job is so complex, the small intestine is assisted by chemicals secreted by two glands that lie outside the alimentary canal: the liver and the pancreas.

The Liver

In an adult, the liver weighs about three to four pounds and lies on the right side, nestled against the diaphragm. It is the only organ that receives its blood supply from two different sources: Arteries deliver about one-fifth of its blood from the heart; the rest (which is rich in digested nutrients) comes from the small intestine by way of a portal vein.

The liver performs more than 500 different jobs as part of several body systems. It purifies the blood of both old red cells and a whole range of poisonous substances, including alcohol. It also manufactures proteins needed by blood plasma. In addition, the liver is the central organ of metabolism, the chemical activities that occur within cells.

The liver acts as the chemical dispatch center for the digestive system by receiving digested food, which it stores, repacks, and releases as the body demands it. For this reason, the liver is an essential adjunct to the digestive system. It assists in the proper use of the nutrients that have traveled through and been processed by the alimentary canal.

The main contribution made by the liver to the digestive process is to manufacture bile, a fluid that is instrumental in the digestion of fat. Bile contains no digestive enzymes but is composed of bile salts, special chemicals that emulsify fats. The liver secretes bile to the gallbladder, a small bag located under the liver. Next, the common bile duct—a tube that passes through the liver's entryway—conveys the fluid from the gallbladder to the small intestine.

Bile, which is not an enzyme, effects no chemical change in fat. Rather, when it reaches the small intestine, bile emulsifies, or breaks down, large globules of fats or oils into tiny globules. This process readies them for the work done later by chemical enzymes. The liver produces more than a pint of bile each day, but only one-tenth of that amount is stored in the gallbladder. Bile is released into the small intestine as needed.

Bile salts are highly alkaline, which means they are the chemical opposite of acid and can neutralize acids into inactivity. Just as hydrochloric acid neutralizes amylase, so bile salts neutralize acids that enter the duodenum (part of the small intestine) from the stomach. At the same time, bile is needed by enzymes in the stomach just as pepsin needs hydrochloric acid. Its alkaline character enables intestinal enzymes to do their jobs.

The Pancreas

The pancreas, another gland that secretes digestive juices into the small intestine, is a boneless, fatless organ, and the second largest gland in the body. It weighs about three ounces, lies in back of the abdomen—

behind part of the stomach—and is joined to the small intestine by the pancreatic duct, a tube that channels secretions whose total weight, in any given hour, equals that of the pancreas itself.

Every 24 hours, the pancreas sends 1 to 2 pints of digestive enzymes through the pancreatic duct into the duodenum. These juices help break down proteins, carbohydrates, and fats. The main protein-digesting enzyme is trypsin, which breaks large protein molecules into smaller units, known as polypeptides, that are then broken down into peptides.

Pancreatic juices also contain large amounts of amylase (an enzyme also present in saliva) that continue the process whereby starch changes to sugar. Pancreatic amylase, which is stronger than salivary amylase, can break down raw starch and other less digestible forms of starch. Lipase, a third pancreatic enzyme, changes emulsified fats to fatty acids and glycerols.

THE SMALL INTESTINE

Although the liver and pancreas secrete important chemicals, most digestion takes place in the small intestine. This coiled and folded organ is the longest part of the alimentary canal and fits neatly into the abdomen. It is about 18- to 21-feet long and has a diameter of about 1½ inches. Its job is to complete all digestion and provide for the absorption of digested nutrients into the bloodstream.

Various sections of the small intestine are known by special names. The first 10 or 12 inches is the C-shaped duodenum, the next 8 or 9 feet is the jejunum, and the remaining length, which connects to the large intestine, is the ileum. While food sits in the small intestine, it is chemically changed by bile sent from the gallbladder and enzymes sent from the pancreas. Food is diluted further by digestive juices produced by the intestinal glands. Every day, the intestine secretes 5 to 10 quarts of intestinal juices. Their chemical action takes about five hours to change all the nutrients in food to their final, cell-ready form.

Microscopic, tubelike glands that line the small intestine also secrete chemicals that are important to digestion. Chyme enters and stretches the walls of the intestine and triggers these glands to release their juices. Like the gastric glands, intestinal glands also produce a thick mucous lining that protects the small intestine from digesting itself.

Intestinal juices contain trypsin and a variety of other protein-digesting enzymes that conclude the final breakdown of peptide into single amino acids. Three intestinal enzymes—lactase, sucrase, and maltase—complete the digestion of carbohydrates. These chemicals split double sugars in the intestine into monosaccharides. The resulting simple sugars, such as glucose, are now ready for absorption into the blood. In addition to playing a vital role in the final digestion of proteins and carbohydrates, intestinal juice also contains more lipase, which is used to complete the change of any remaining fats.

The five hours of activity in the duodenum mark the end of chemical digestion: Carbohydrates are changed to simple sugars, proteins are changed to simple amino acids, and fats become fatty acids and glycerol. These digestive end products move on to the jejunum for absorption into the bloodstream. From this second section of the small intestine, most of the digested nutrients pass out of the alimentary canal.

The walls of the small intestine are folded over many times and are lined with millions of tiny, fingerlike villi. These villi provide the small intestine with a surface area of more than 600 square yards that may be used to absorb digested nutrients. This is comparable to the floor size of a room 60 yards long and 10 yards wide. In fact, the surface area of the small intestine is about 10 times greater than the surface area of the skin.

The villi do their job by waving back and forth and capturing digested nutrients that, by peristaltic action, move through the small intestine in a soupy paste. Each villus contains a network of blood capillaries and a lacteal, a projection of the lymph system. Each villus is covered with a single layer of cells that have tiny openings, or pores, between them. Digested nutrients pass through the pores and into the microscopic vessels inside: Amino acids and simple sugars pass into the blood capillaries; fat nutrients, which are screened out of the blood tubes, pass into the lacteal. After passing into the lymph system, fats make their way through a large lymph duct into the bloodstream. Vitamins and minerals pass unchanged from the small intestine into the blood or lymph. All the nutrients that have traveled through the digestive tract finally reach the body's stream of circulating blood.

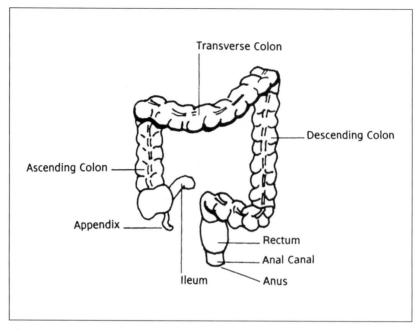

Figure 4: *The large intestine.*

THE LARGE INTESTINE

The large intestine, or colon, is about five- to six-feet long and about two and a half inches in diameter. Its joint with the ileum is a T-shaped connection, at which a portion of the colon—situated to the left of the T—serves no real purpose. This section, which bends downward and is called the cecum, attaches to a thin structure known as the appendix. The two- to six-inch-long appendix serves no evident purpose. Some experts—such as the award-winning science writer David Kraus—think it may have been of use to prehistoric humans whose crude diet required the services of a special organ that could digest dense fiber such as tree bark. More recent research is investigating the possibility that the appendix plays a yet undiscovered role in the body's immune system.

The large intestine rises upward (the part of the organ called the ascending colon), turns and crosses to the left of the abdomen above the first folds of the small intestine (the transverse colon). It then bends downward again (the descending colon) on the left side, circling in to join the rectum. This muscular end of the large intestine leads to the outside of the body through the anus.

Although no digestion of food occurs in the large intestine, it reabsorbs into the bloodstream water (and whatever vitamins and minerals it contains) added to the alimentary canal during the digestive process. The main job of the large intestine, however, is to transport waste materials out of the body.

Most of the material that moves into the colon forms feces, the waste products of digestion. In the colon, peristalsis will slowly propel feces toward the anus, which opens to the outside of the body. Millions of harmless (and often useful) bacteria, called intestinal flora, live in the large intestine. These organisms combine with undigested matter to form 10% to 50% of the feces. The remainder is largely water, cellulose, fiber, unprocessed nutrients, and mucus. Together, these wastes are pushed forward toward the rectum, where they may be stored for as long as 24 hours before being excreted. By the time the large intestine has discharged the remains of one meal, it has already begun to receive new undigested matter and water from the small intestine. Like the other digestive organs, the colon stays on the job as long as food continues to enter the alimentary canal.

THE SYSTEM SUMMED UP

Once the digestive system has finished its work, the nutrients that have passed into the bloodstream undergo further preparation before they are used by individual body cells. The chief responsibility for the processing of absorbed materials belongs to the liver. This extraordinary gland receives the end products of digestion through the stomach and the small intestine.

Amino acids pass through the liver and are hastened into the blood for delivery to other organs. About 10% of the fatty acids and glycerol in the intestine also travel through the liver, which changes them to fatty substances called lipids. One of the more familiar lipids, cholesterol, is found in almost every cell in the body.

The simple sugars that leave the small intestine are stored by the liver in the form of glycogen, or animal starch. Stored sugar can be broken down to release glucose into the blood when it is needed for energy by the cells. Muscles in the body use blood glucose to produce their own glycogen. They use the glycogen, in turn, as a reserve store of fuel and can break it down again rapidly when the body needs a quick supply of energy. The liver, then, vitally assists the digestive system by receiving and distributing the nutrients necessary for keeping the body healthy and functional.

The digestive system works largely without any conscious help; it is an autonomous bodily system. Once swallowed, valuable nutrients and their food packaging are automatically moved, step by step, through the esophagus, the stomach, and the intestines. They are sorted, separated, and simplified by an efficient, specialized system that operates every hour of every day, for as long as we live. This system is vulnerable, however, to a number of disorders. And they are the next part of the story.

5

DIGESTIVE DISORDERS

La Colique, *by Honoré Daumier, illustrates the agony of indigestion.*

F ew people realize how many disorders affect the digestive tract. In the United States, one out of six major illnesses involves the digestive system. Each year, more than 5 million patients enter hospitals for treatment of a digestive disorder. Americans spend more than $500 million on nonprescription digestion medications. In fact, digestive disorders are so widespread that they surpass the common cold as the leading cause of absenteeism in the country's industries.

There are several reasons why the digestive system is prone to disorders. First, the system includes many organs. Second, it performs many complex functions. Third, it is among the more sensitive systems of the body, vulnerable not only to bacterial invasion but also to problems caused by diet and stress.

Luckily, most digestive disorders respond well to medical treatment and to fairly simple preventive measures that most of us can take.

DISORDERS OF THE MOUTH

Disorders that affect the mouth, the first organ of digestion, can inhibit our ingestion of food. One ailment that occurs often is stomatitis, an inflammation of the mouth characterized by tenderness, swelling, and redness. Glossitis is a form of stomatitis that affects the tongue, whereas gingivitis affects the gums. Both maladies can cause bad breath and an excess production of saliva. Aphthous stomatitis, or mouth ulcers, is an especially troublesome condition. Its symptoms include the appearance of small, painful white blisters anywhere in the mouth. Many forms of mouth inflammation can be treated with mouthwashes and creams, but if stomatitis continues for more than a few days, a doctor should be consulted.

Disorders of the mouth, such as gum disease, can damage the teeth and make eating painful.

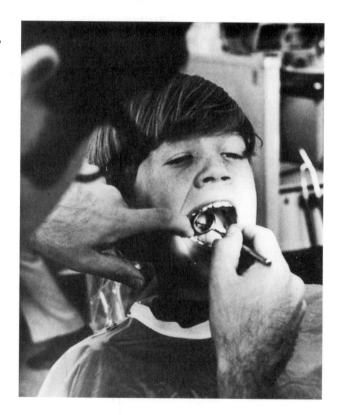

Teeth play a vital role in preparing food for further digestion. And most people recognize that their teeth should be in good repair. Many of us, however, do not understand the importance of healthy gums. Indeed, the main threat to the teeth is gum disease, which occurs as commonly as tooth decay. It is often caused by bacterial plaque that sticks to the base of teeth. Very sore, bleeding gums—they may turn red and bluish purple— indicate gingivitis. If inflamed gums are not treated, teeth may loosen and shift, and eating may become painful and difficult.

Inflamed membranes at the roots of the teeth indicate periodontal disease. Bacterial plaque buildup can also result in this condition, which can cause sensitive gums to develop pus and to recede from the surface of the tooth. Persistent gum problems can often be effectively treated by a periodontist, or gum specialist.

DISORDERS OF THE ESOPHAGUS

Once food is swallowed, it must pass through the esophagus to the stomach. Disorders of the throat or esophagus may cause dysphagia, or difficulty in swallowing. Sometimes a swallowed substance (or a foreign object) can damage the lining of the esophagus and cause swallowing to be painful and difficult. Whenever the lining of the esophagus becomes inflamed, the condition is called esophagitis. Several factors can create this inflammation, including hot irritating foods, smoking, severe vomiting, or infections.

The most common inflammation of the esophagus is *reflux esophagitis,* or heartburn, a burning sensation in the middle of the chest that usually occurs right after eating. Millions of people experience this discomfort from time to time. Its source is the sphincter muscle that separates the esophagus from the stomach. Under normal circumstances, the sphincter opens to allow food into the stomach and then closes immediately to prevent any contents from flowing back into the esophagus. If the sphincter fails to do its job properly, hydrochloric acid from the stomach can back up and irritate the walls of the esophagus.

A liquid antacid usually relieves the pain of occasional heartburn, but not in the case of people who have chronic esophagitis, the result of a weak sphincter that regularly allows stomach acid, and even bile, to flow back into the esophagus. If untreated, chronic esophagitis can scar the esophagus. Such damage may make swallowing very difficult and even impossible.

Tumors also sometimes develop in the esophagus, though they are usually benign (noncancerous). But cancer can infect the cells that line the esophagus. It happens more often in men than women and in blacks more often than whites. Esophageal cancer appears to be not hereditary but rather cultural: It is more widespread in Japan, for instance, than in the United States. Researchers are currently investigating the Japanese diet and related matters for clues that may help explain that nation's high incidence of esophageal cancer.

Just above the stomach, the esophagus passes through the diaphragm—the muscular membrane that separates the organs of the abdomen from the organs of the chest. Sometimes, a small opening appears where the esophagus meets the stomach. If a small part of the stomach slides upward into this opening, hiatal hernia develops. Someone with this condition may suffer chest pains after eating, and the pains sharpen when the victim lies down or coughs. Stomach acid may spill back into the esophagus and cause bleeding. A hiatal hernia may require surgery, but it is often treated by a change in diet to small meals free of gasproducing foods.

DISORDERS OF THE STOMACH

Like the lining of the esophagus, the mucous lining of the stomach is vulnerable to irritation. The effects of gastritis, or inflammation of the stomach lining, range from slight discomfort to chronic, debilitating pain.

A person with gastritis may experience nausea, vomiting, abdominal discomfort, loss of appetite, bloating, and diarrhea. Gastritis can also cause bleeding (which may show up in vomit) or the passage of black stools. When gastritis results from an irritant such as alcohol or aspirin, it is usually felt soon after the sufferer swallows the substance. Once the irritating substances leave the stomach—either naturally or by pumping—mild cases of gastritis normally are relieved.

Gastroenteritis is an inflammatory condition of the lining of the stomach and the intestine caused by infections or food poisoning. The symptoms of this disorder—nausea, vomiting, abdominal cramping and tenderness, and diarrhea—appear suddenly and without warning. Doctors treat gastroenteritis by recommending that the patient rest in bed and begin a restricted diet.

At one time or another, roughly 1 person in 10 suffers an ulcer, a break in the mucous membrane or skin of an organ that results in an open sore. A peptic ulcer is one that appears in the stomach or the duodenum. If it appears within the stomach it is called a gastric ulcer, which is a specific type of peptic ulcer. Gastric ulcers, which affect men and women alike, may vary in size from microscopic to more than an inch in diameter, though the size of an ulcer has no bearing on the discomfort it causes. People afflicted with ulcers usually feel pain in the upper abdomen after they eat. The source of this pain is not only the ulcer itself but also excess acid in the stomach and, in some instances, an irritation of the entire stomach lining.

In order for an ulcer to heal, the victim must lower the quantity of gastric acids and pepsin he or she secretes. Medications used to help control gastric secretions include antacids, histamine H_2 receptor

A laboratory technician checks a shipment of Tagamet, a drug approved by the Federal Drug Administration in 1988 for the treatment of ulcers.

Physicians advise ulcer sufferers to avoid tobacco and alcohol, both of which slow healing and cause recurrences.

antagonists, and prostaglandins. Physicians advise ulcer sufferers to avoid tobacco and alcohol, which slow the proper healing of ulcers and cause them to recur. Aspirin and other nonsteroidal anti-inflammatory drugs, which can irritate the stomach lining, should also be avoided.

In extreme cases, the ulcer will erode blood vessels, which may bleed profusely and cause shock or even death. A bleeding ulcer can burn a hole that extends all the way through the stomach wall, allowing the contents of the stomach to spill out. When this occurs, surgery is needed to drain and close the opening.

Approximately 20,000 people each year in the United States are diagnosed as having stomach cancer. Twice as many men develop this disease as do women, and the condition occurs most often among people over 50. The countries with the highest incidence of stomach cancer are Japan, China, and Iceland.

The symptoms of stomach cancer resemble those of peptic ulcers. Unlike ulcer pain, however, the gnawing pain of stomach cancer does not lessen after meals. Sometimes no symptoms occur until blockage appears at the opening of the stomach to the small intestine. Doctors cannot al-

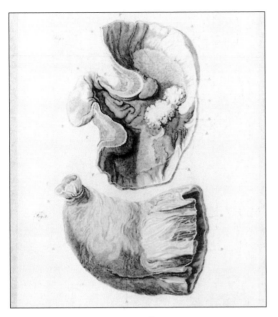

A drawing illustrates a side-view cross section of a cancerous stomach. Doctors will often treat stomach cancer by performing a gastrectomy, an operation in which all or part of the stomach is removed.

ways treat stomach cancer. When they can, they perform a gastrectomy, a surgical procedure whereby part or all of the stomach is removed.

Because the stomach is not absolutely vital to digestion, patients can survive a gastrectomy in good health, eat fairly goodsized meals, and lead a relatively normal life. They may need injections of vitamin B_{12} and iron, though, because a stomach that has been partly or entirely removed cannot perform the important task of absorbing some vitamins and minerals.

DISORDERS OF THE LIVER, GALLBLADDER, AND PANCREAS

Disorders that occur in the liver, gallbladder, and pancreas can hinder both digestion and nourishment. The most common disease of the liver is viral hepatitis, which is caused by one of three closely related viruses that are transmitted to the liver in different ways.

Hepatitis

Infectious hepatitis (Type A) is a contagious disease that most commonly infects children and young adults. It is spread through contact with feces contaminated with hepatitis A virus. It takes about two weeks before symptoms appear.

The symptoms of infectious hepatitis include fever, headache, loss of appetite, nausea, vomiting, and diarrhea or constipation. The patient's feces are often pale because they lack bile, which is blocked from leaving the liver. At the same time, the victim may develop jaundice, a yellowing of the skin and the whites of the eyes. This condition is caused by an accumulation of a dark-yellow bile pigment in the blood; it also indicates, however, that the patient has begun to recover. Bed rest is the best treatment for hepatitis A, which normally immunizes the victim for life against any subsequent attack by the virus.

Hepatitis B lasts longer and does more harm. Formerly, this disease was known as serum hepatitis, because it was often transmitted through contaminated blood transfusions. Today, blood is screened to detect the presence of the hepatitis B virus, but the disease can be spread through a variety of skin punctures such as those caused by intravenous drug use and accidental syringe pricks in hospitals. The hepatitis B virus lives in the body fluids of an infected person and can be spread through sexual contact.

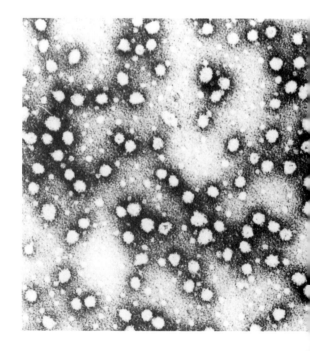

A photomicrograph of the hepatitis B virus. Hepatitis B—a sometimes fatal disorder—can be transmitted through sexual contact.

The symptoms of hepatitis B are the same as those for hepatitis A—only more intense. The incubation period lasts from two to six months instead of two to six weeks. During this time, hepatitis B is most contagious, although the victim may continue to be a carrier of the virus even after his or her own symptoms disappear. The virus survives until the body produces special chemicals, called antibodies, that fight it off. Producing the antibodies, which eventually offer immunity against the virus, can take many years. A vaccine is available for persons at high risk of contracting hepatitis B, such as health care workers or family members of the infected person.

Hepatitis C, formerly called non-A, non-B hepatitis, is the most frequent cause of chronic hepatitis. It is usually spread through contact with infected blood. The symptoms are similar to those of hepatitis B. More than half of those with hepatitis C, however, develops chronic infections, which can result in cirrhosis. The antiviral agent alpha-interferon may be used to treat the inflammation of chronic hepatitis.

Cirrhosis

Each year over 25,000 people in the United States die of cirrhosis, a chronic liver disorder often caused by alcoholism. Cirrhosis may also be caused by previous infections, toxins, or malnutrition. In cirrhosis, scarring, or fibrosis, hampers the normal functioning of the liver, which becomes permanently and progressively damaged. A cirrhotic liver may continue to function, but serious problems may result as the scar tissue blocks the free flow of blood to and from the organ.

Cirrhosis cripples the liver's ability to destroy invading bacteria and can stop its production of a protein that keeps plasma inside the blood vessels. It can also prevent the liver from detoxifying ammonia, that is, from changing it into a safe substance; in its original state, ammonia that enters the nervous system can prove fatal.

Cholecystitis

Cholecystitis is the medical term for gallbladder trouble. Cholelithiasis, or the production of gallstones, is a common disorder of the gallbladder, and gallstones obstruct the free flow of bile. It is estimated that 20% of the population of Americans over 65 years old are afflicted with gallstones.

Most gallstones are composed of a hard cholesterol mass that may form in the gallbladder or in the common bile duct connected to the small intestine. This mass blocks the duct and inflames the gallbladder.

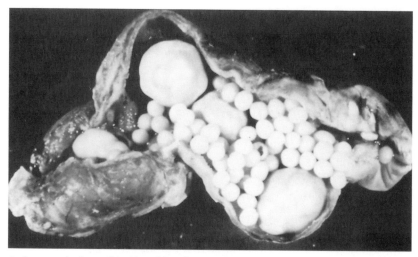

A photograph of a gallbladder with gallstones. This disorder is most commonly treated with an operation that surgically removes the gallbladder and clears out the bile duct.

The organ then suffers an attack that causes a severe pain in the right upper abdomen as well as nausea, vomiting, and fever.

The most common treatment is surgical removal of the gallbladder and clearing out of the bile duct. The gallbladder is not an essential organ and so it can be removed with no ill effects. Indeed, surgical removal of the gallbladder is one of the most common types of abdominal operation performed on older people in the United States. The duct itself is needed to transport bile from the liver and so cannot be removed.

Sometimes no surgery is necessary because the stones that have blocked the duct dissolve or simply pass out of the body. They may leave a trail of damage, however, that produces inflammation, infection, and pus within the gallbladder. Infection of the gallbladder must be diagnosed and treated early to avoid serious, and possibly fatal, complications.

Pancreatitis

Pancreatitis is an inflammation of the pancreas cells that secrete digestive juices. If the digestive enzymes from the pancreas empty into the abdominal cavity, they may severely inflame the peritoneum, the membrane that lines this area. Unless this condition, known as peritonitis, is treated, death may result.

Pancreatitis causes severe pain and tenderness in the upper middle and left parts of the abdomen. Other symptoms include nausea, vomiting, loss of appetite, constipation, fever, heart palpitations, and clammy skin.

DISORDERS OF THE SMALL INTESTINE

Ulcers

As excess digestive juices sometimes eat away at the lining of the stomach, an overproduction of these acids may pour into the duodenum, causing a duodenal ulcer. All ulcers produce pain in the upper abdomen, but the pain of a duodenal ulcer begins when the stomach is empty and wanes after the patient has eaten a small meal. Duodenal ulcer pain recurs in the middle of the night, when stomach acid levels reach their peak.

Duodenal ulcers are the most common ulcers in the digestive tract. Medication can often improve them, but untreated ulcerous conditions can develop four serious complications: bleeding, obstruction, perforation, and intractability. The greatest number of deaths from ulcerous conditions are caused by acute perforations, erosions that penetrate the wall of the duodenum (or the stomach). As a result the contents of the digestive organ spill into the abdominal cavity, often causing severe and dangerous infections.

An intractable ulcer is one that returns very rapidly even after it has healed. It does not respond to ordinary medications and often must be treated with surgery. A person who has, or suspects he or she has, an ulcer should see a doctor for proper attention. Unfortunately, many people with ulcers continue to put stock in groundless folk wisdom, such as the notion that drinking milk will relieve an ulcer and eating spices will aggravate one. It is true, however, that anyone with an ulcer should avoid alcohol, cola, coffee, aspirin, and tobacco, which are all strong acid producers and potential irritants. It is also true that avoiding these substances can prevent some ulcers from forming and may help stop an existing ulcer from worsening.

Crohn's Disease

Another inflammation that can affect the small intestine is called Crohn's disease, ileitis, or regional enteritis, which seems to strike children and young adults more often than it does any other age group. This ailment causes small nodules, or masses of tissue, to become inflamed and to penetrate deeply into the walls of the intestine. Abdominal cramps ensue, along with diarrhea, fever, and weight loss. As the disease develops, fistulas—unnatural passageways—form. Infected materials may pass from the intestine through the fistulas and affect nearby organs.

Inflammation of the intestine is treated with bed rest and a special diet. In some instances, antibiotics have helped reduce the inflammation, but as yet no cure for this debilitating disease has been found.

Hernia

Another disorder that can affect the small intestine is a hernia, a condition that occurs when a tissue or organ moves out of position and pushes against those nearby. Sometimes, a part of the intestine pushes out through a gap in the muscle wall of the abdomen. Many men develop an inguinal hernia, which develops in the groin and may extend into the scrotum, the external sac that holds the testicles. This hernia forms from part of the small intestine and lies in front of the connecting tissue that separates the thigh and the abdomen at the groin. Hernias can result from severe muscle strain in lifting heavy objects, coughing, or moving the bowels. In many cases, a hernia requires surgery.

DISORDERS OF THE LARGE INTESTINE
Irritable Bowel Syndrome

At least half of all the ailments that occur within the digestive system result from a single disorder, irritable bowel syndrome, also known as spastic colon, functional dyspepsia, or nervous indigestion. This condition, often caused by emotional stress and anxiety, includes a wide variety of symptoms.

Some people with irritable bowel syndrome feel a cramping pain in the middle and lower abdomen. The pain sometimes spreads across the chest and shoulders. The abdomen may bloat, and the person may suffer nausea, headache, loss of appetite, fatigue, and alternating periods of diarrhea and constipation.

Diarrhea, the passing of soft or watery stool, is a symptom, not a disease. It may be caused by stress, bacterial or viral infections, changes in diet, or inflammations of the colon. It can also be a side effect of an antibiotic. Prolonged diarrhea may dehydrate the body, and the ailment should never be ignored.

Constipation is the difficult or infrequent elimination of waste from the large intestine. It, too, may be a symptom of a disease or caused by stress. It sometimes occurs when there is not enough fiber in the diet. Like diarrhea, a change in diet or the use of medications can cause constipation. A person with severe or longterm constipation should see a doctor to make sure there is no obstruction in the colon.

People with irritable bowel syndrome are usually given medication. Bed rest may also help. Because this syndrome is often caused by emotional stress, symptoms can disappear if the patient's anxiety is eased.

Hemorrhoids, Colitis, and Diverticulosis

Chronic constipation sometimes causes enlarged veins near the anus, called hemorrhoids. When these veins dilate, they cause severe inflammation that leads to intense itching, bleeding, and discomfort. Most hemorrhoids can be treated by medications that reduce their itching and swelling. If symptoms remain for more than a few days, a doctor should be consulted.

Colitis, or inflammation of the colon, often besets people in their twenties and thirties. The most common form of this disorder, which is called ulcerative colitis, usually develops slowly. Its symptoms include abdominal cramps, a constant urge to defecate, and bloody stools. As colitis progresses, the victim may suffer fever, weight loss, and a general feeling of illness.

The cause of this disease is unknown, but doctors believe stress may be a factor. The condition is serious and must receive medical treatment; if it does not, complications may affect other organs. A victim of colitis may be in danger of bleeding severely, and requires bed rest and a very strict diet. Medication can help relieve the symptoms of colitis, but severe cases sometimes require the removal of the diseased part of the large intestine.

Diverticulosis is a condition in which a small sac of mucous membrane projects through a weak section of the intestinal wall. The appearance of these small pouches, or diverticula, causes pain and upsets the regularity of bowel movements. In a more advanced stage of the disease, the colon wall thickens and becomes inflamed. The thick mass remains infected, further inflammation sets in, and materials that move through the colon may be blocked.

Symptoms of diverticulosis include severe pain in the lower left side and the lower back. The patient feels nauseated, may experience both constipation and diarrhea, and can also develop a chill and fever.

Diverticulosis often clears up when fiber is added to the patient's diet. Physicians may also prescribe antibiotics to clear up the infection, and patients can take medications to relieve the constipation or diarrhea.

Cancer

Cancer of the colon and rectum (colorectal cancer) is one of the most common types of cancer. Some victims suffer no symptoms at all, but about two-thirds of all patients experience pain, vomiting, weight loss, and a change in bowel movements.

A high-fiber diet may help prevent colon cancer. In addition, early detection of this disease plays a vital part in successful treatment.

The best treatment for cancer of the colon and rectum is the complete removal of the affected part of the colon. Often, when the cancerous section is removed, the remainder of the colon is left intact. In some cases, a colostomy may have to be performed. During this procedure, a surgeon makes an artificial hole in the wall of the abdomen so that the colon opens directly to the outside of the body. Sometimes, a colostomy is a temporary procedure. In such cases, when the blockage is cleared, the colon can be reattached to the rectum.

When the entire colon must be disconnected for a time or removed, a similar procedure, called an ileostomy, may be in order. In this surgery, the ileum, or end of the small intestine, is brought through the wall of the abdomen.

A person who has had a colostomy or an ileostomy cannot defecate in the normal way. Instead, feces are passed into a bag attached to the surface of the abdomen. Once a patient has learned how to change the bags, and to adjust to the surgery that has taken place, he or she can control bowel movements. Other people cannot detect the artificial anus, and colostomy patients usually find that their personal life is very much the same as it was before.

Appendicitis

Sometimes the appendix, which extends from the beginning of the large intestine, becomes blocked and inflamed. When this condition, called appendicitis, occurs, the appendix swells and blocks off the supply of oxygen and nutrients that normally reach it. As the condition worsens, the cells of the appendix die and may become gangrenous, or highly infected. If this decaying tissue perforates, or bursts, its contents spill into the abdominal cavity. Untreated appendicitis develops into peritonitis, a fatal ailment.

The first symptom of appendicitis is pain around the navel, followed by constipation, nausea, and vomiting. After a few hours, the pain usually moves to the lower right side of the abdomen. Fever may occur, and the pulse rate may quicken. The higher the fever, and the worse the pain, the greater the possibility that the appendix will rupture. All these symptoms indicate a medical emergency.

An inflamed appendix is surgically removed because surgery puts the patient at much lower risk than do the infection and danger that follow a perforated appendix.

AN OUNCE OF PREVENTION

Many people do not know how to recognize and get early medical attention for digestive problems. As a result, they may undergo unnecessary suffering and anxiety. In fact, there is a wide range of special tests and instruments that can help diagnose disorders of the digestive tract.

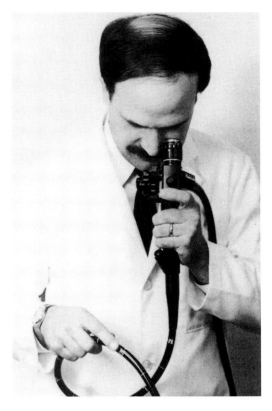

A physician uses an endoscope, a device that enables doctors to view the interior of hollow organs such as the alimentary canal.

The fiberoptic endoscope, for example, affords a view of areas of the alimentary canal from the esophagus to the anus. Technicians use this apparatus to take photographs, motion pictures, and videotapes of the digestive tract. It can even be used to remove small tissue samples and to perform minor operations.

The digestive system processes and absorbs materials that make all human activity possible. Understanding what may go wrong is an essential step in keeping this vital system in good operating order, and in keeping yourself well-nourished and healthy.

6

THE ROAD TO GOOD DIGESTION

At some time or another, almost everyone experiences a touch of discomfort after eating, a condition commonly referred to as indigestion and known medically as dyspepsia. This condition describes a variety of symptoms resulting from an inability to use or absorb the foods we eat. Symptoms can appear alone or in combination. One person may feel a mild pain in the upper abdomen or a sensation of heartburn. Another may experience bloating. Still another may suffer nausea or diarrhea.

In any case, indigestion signals that somewhere in the digestive tract, food is having trouble making its way through the system. The trouble may begin with the food itself if it is too rich in fats, for instance, or poorly cooked. It can be the price a person pays for eating too much or too quickly. It even can be caused by eating in an unpleasant environment, and very often is the response of the digestive system to anxiety and stress.

STRESS AND DIGESTION

When a person is tense or anxious, the digestive system can suffer the punishment. Many people react to stress by eating more than they should and more rapidly. Others, in whom the digestive process has slowed, lose their appetite and may become nauseated at the very thought of food. They feel full and heavy even though they have not eaten for a long time. Both these extremes show how stress can dramatically interfere with good digestion.

Eating moderate amounts of food at a leisurely pace in pleasant surroundings is one way of ensuring good digestion. Another way is to exercise certain precautions. It is a good idea, for example, not to smoke, because doing so irritates the digestive system. It is also a good idea not

A cozy French bistro has the right atmosphere for relaxed dining for President Clinton, First Lady Hilary Rodham Clinton, French President Jacques Chirac and Chirac's wife Bernadette.

Because exercising too soon after a meal can cause serious stomach cramps, swimmers should wait at least an hour after eating before going into the water.

to engage in any strenuous activity, such as exercise, immediately before or after eating.

Swimming, for example, can put someone at serious risk if he or she enters the water less than one hour after eating. The reason is that digestion and swimming both tax the circulation system. A swimmer who plunges into a pool or lake too soon after a meal, especially if the water is cool, risks developing a stomach cramp, the result of an overtaxed circulation system drawing blood away from the stomach muscles. Such a cramp may make it difficult or impossible to continue the exercise.

Nutrition and Stress

In recent years some direct connections between stress and good nutrition have been established. For example, it is now known that stress prevents the body from properly absorbing and using a number of vital nutrients. Stress can deplete the body of vitamins C, A, and E, as well as calcium, magnesium, zinc, and protein.

The eating habits of teenagers compound the overall stress they often feel. Unbalanced, high-sugar diets can cause fluctuations in blood sugar that put pressure on several body organs, including the pancreas, the liver, and the brain. Good nutrition can minimize anxiety, and the foods a person eats can actually help relieve stress; there are also foods, such as those rich in proteins, that can promote alertness.

In the mid-1980s, Dr. Judith J. Wurtman and her colleagues at the Massachusetts Institute of Technology (MIT) conducted a series of studies on food and mood. Their findings, as well as those in other similar studies, showed that choosing the right food can relieve tension and stimulate more energetic feelings.

The studies centered around neurotransmitters, chemicals that pass messages in the brain from cell to cell. Ten years before these studies were conducted, scientists had discovered that the brain manufactures

Eating habits affect mood and behavior. An excess of foods high in sugar can cause fluctuations in blood sugar and increase stress, whereas a more nutritious diet can minimize anxiety.

three types of neurotransmitters from nutrients contained in foods. Two of the neurotransmitters, the alertness chemicals dopamine and norepinephrine, help us think more quickly and feel more attentive and motivated. Another neurotransmitter, serotonin, is a calming chemical that eases feelings of stress and tension and increases the ability to concentrate.

In her research, Wurtman found that ingesting as little as one or two ounces of carbohydrates can trigger the brain to increase its serotonin production. The extra serotonin calms the nerves. For some reason, people who are 20% or more overweight and women who are about to begin menstruation sometimes require another ounce or two of carbohydrates to feel less anxious.

Sources of stress-relieving carbohydrates include bagels, bread, cereals, low-fat crackers, corn, muffins, pasta, popcorn, and rolls. Because liquids pass through the digestive system more easily than solids, the fastest means of ingesting carbohydrates is to drink them. People whose stress is accompanied by a loss of appetite can sip sweetened tea, decaffeinated soda, or hot cocoa (made with water), through a straw. Sipping, and pausing momentarily between sips, stimulates their relaxing effects much sooner.

Wurtman emphasizes that we should consume stress-relieving snacks slowly and calmly. It is also important to stop eating as soon as the required amount (one to four ounces) is consumed. The purpose of a carbohydrate snack is to stimulate serotonin production, not to satisfy a craving for sweets. Overeating and gaining weight can add to a person's anxiety. But small amounts of carbohydrates enhance the calming effects of serotonin and help ease anxiety, anger, frustration, and other negative feelings.

MEDICATIONS AND DIGESTION

Over-the-counter (OTC) antacids can usually neutralize excess acids safely. It is dangerous to assume, however, that antacid preparations can be taken regularly without risk of incurring ill effects. Overusing antacids, for example, has been shown to deplete the body of phosphorus, a mineral that makes up part of the structure of bone cells. In the digestive tract, antacids combine with phosphates to sweeten a sour stomach. At the same time, the antacids interfere with the proper absorption of phosphorus, leaving the body deficient in an important mineral.

Sodium bicarbonate, or baking soda, is a widely used antacid, and is the main ingredient in many OTC preparations. It often provides relief for minor indigestion but can endanger people who suffer from hypertension, or high blood pressure. People with this condition are advised to restrict their intake of sodium to about 1,000 mg (milligrams) a day. (A regular dose of antacid medication contains 1,042 ma; the body actually needs no more than 200 mg to function properly.) Label instructions usually suggest that antacids may be taken four times a day. A person with high blood pressure who ingests even a single dose may be in real trouble. Long-term use of baking-soda remedies, even by those with normal blood pressure, is not advisable.

Other popular OTC antacids, such as Alka-Seltzer, contain sodium bicarbonate and aspirin. Aspirin, the most common painkiller in the United States, is often used in medications that promise to relieve gastric distress. But aspirin, or acetylsalicylic acid, is known to irritate the stomach and may cause stomach bleeding. Thus, although the bicarbonate in such medications soothes the acid irritation, the aspirin makes it worse.

Calcium carbonate is another ingredient often found in heartburn remedies. The regular use of calcium carbonate can lead to constipation, however. There is also evidence that large amounts of this chemical may, in fact, cause the stomach to secrete more acid after three or four hours have passed. This leads to another dose of the medication, which leads to more heartburn, which leads to the need for more medication—and the cycle can continue indefinitely.

Another common ingredient in antacids is aluminum hydroxide. Like calcium carbonate, it may cause constipation. However, most remedies (such as Maalox and Mylanta) that contain aluminum also contain magnesium, which acts as a laxative and counteracts the constipating tendency of aluminum. As with all OTC medications, problems can be avoided if consumers do not overuse the product.

Antacids can also create difficulties for people who are already taking medications for other disorders. Antacids may seriously interfere with the absorption of some medications and decrease their therapeutic effects. For example, aluminum antacids can reduce the absorption of digitalis heart medicines. They also decrease the absorption of iron supplements given to people with anemia and of some drugs taken by people with tuberculosis. Some major tranquilizers lose their effectiveness if taken with antacids, as do a long list of tetracycline antibiotics.

Tetracycline drugs often cause indigestion. The urge to take an antacid is understandable, but it can keep the antibiotic from doing its job. A good rule is to avoid taking an antacid within two hours of taking any other medication.

Anyone who uses an antacid should read the label carefully. It is a federal law that all labels include warnings against the use of a particular product by people afflicted with specific conditions, such as hypertension. The label will also indicate that prolonged or regular use of any antacid may be dangerous. Symptoms of indigestion that remain for an extended time may indicate a more serious condition, and should be diagnosed by a physician. Heart attack symptoms, for instance, are often mistaken for indigestion. Ordinary symptoms of indigestion usually are not serious, and under proper conditions, the careful, moderate use of antacids may, indeed, provide relief.

FOODS AND MEDICATIONS

The basis of good digestion is healthy foods and liquids. But even the most nourishing substances may hamper the effects of prescription medicine. Many patients are not warned sufficiently about the possibly harmful interaction of food and medications. Consider the way in which a tablet or capsule should be taken: Few people can swallow a pill without liquid. Consequently, they often reach for a drink that is close at hand or one they find tasty.

This seems harmless enough, but, in fact, the choice of liquid may prove to be important. Fruit and vegetable juices and carbonated sodas are all acid drinks. As such, they curtail the effectiveness of many antibiotics, including ampicillin, erythromycin, and penicillin. Milk is also a poor choice. It does not mix with iron, and does not allow bisacodyl laxatives to dissolve. These laxatives should not be taken within an hour of drinking milk or taking antacids. Milk also interferes with the proper absorption of tetracycline antibiotics. It blocks them from reaching the bloodstream properly and doing their jobs effectively. Milk is good for some drugs, however. Aspirin is less of a stomach irritant if taken with a full glass of milk. The same is true of strong arthritis remedies that often cause gastric problems.

The best swallowing aid is plain water. Not only is water generally noninteractive, but it often sweeps high concentrations of the medication into the bloodstream. An eight-ounce glass of water helps medicines both to dissolve properly and to be absorbed in their required amounts.

Many people take medications without knowing whether they should be taken with food or on an empty stomach. Like liquids, solid foods can block the absorption of medications, though some foods have the opposite effect. In addition, some medications can cause severe gastric problems if they are taken with foods, whereas others are powerful irritants if taken on an empty stomach.

A number of arthritis medications, such as Motrin, can cause pain, nausea, vomiting, diarrhea, and ulcers if taken on an empty stomach. On the other hand, ampicillin and erythromycin cause stomach distress if taken after food has entered the stomach. A high-carbohydrate meal may retard the absorption of a painkiller such as Tylenol, whereas a high-fat dinner will help absorb a fungus medication such as Fulvicin. Information about the proper way to take a medication should come from the prescribing doctor or the pharmacist. Anyone who must take medication should ask for clear and specific instructions about when and how the medication should be taken.

If a drug is to be taken "on an empty stomach," it usually means at least one hour before meals or two hours after. "With meals"— which generally means just before, during, or after eating—does not mean with a snack. Medications that are to be taken with food need a full stomach. Food may lessen potential irritation to the stomach or prevent the nausea and vomiting that are side effects of many medications. If no instructions are available, medications should be taken with a full glass of water on an empty stomach.

TRAVELER'S DIARRHEA

The most common illness among travelers who leave their native country is an assault on the digestive tract that causes severe diarrhea. Traveler's diarrhea is caused by bacteria-contaminated food. Substandard sanitary conditions and unfamiliar foods can bring on diarrhea with its resulting dehydration, weakness, and fatigue.

The general rules for preventing traveler's diarrhea are known to most experienced tourists: When in another country use only boiled or bottled water, not only in foods but also for cleaning teeth. (Watch out for ice served in drinks.) Never drink locally bottled water. Eat only well-cooked foods that have not been left standing for more than 15 minutes. Boil milk or cream, and ask for boiled milk or cream for coffee when in a restaurant. Never eat raw cheese or foods sold by street vendors. Peel all raw fruits and vegetables.

Nevertheless, even the most seasoned traveler can become a victim of traveler's diarrhea. Although prescription medications such as Lomotil will relieve the symptoms once the disease has set in, it may be possible to prevent traveler's diarrhea from occurring.

Dr. Herbert Dupont, a gastroenterologist at the University of Texas Medical School at Houston, studied the disorder among a group of students attending summer classes in Guadalajara, Mexico. He found that students who took 2 ounces a day of *bismuth subsaticylate* (Pepto Bismol) for 21 days experienced fewer intestinal problems, and were less likely to come down with diarrhea, than those who did not take the medication daily. In addition, none of the students who participated in the study suffered any adverse side effects from the bismuth subsalicylate.

Tourists can avoid the discomfort of "travelers' diarrhea" by taking certain precautions, such as taking bismuth subsalicylate, before embarking on a journey outside of the United States.

Traveler's diarrhea appears within 2 to 10 days of the visitor's being in a new area. The high-risk locations include Latin America, Asia, Africa, Eastern Europe, and some Mediterranean countries. Dr. Dupont's study indicates that the bismuth subsalicylate ingredient in Pepto Bismol may offer many wary travelers a safe means of preventing this debilitating condition.

EAT WELL—FEEL WELL

If you wake up tired in the morning, even after a good night's sleep, you may be feeling the effects of low blood sugar in your body. Most probably, a person who has slept well but then has difficulty in waking up ate the wrong food at or near bedtime the night before. Contrary to what you might think, low-blood sugar follows the ingestion of sweets and prevents the body and brain from responding properly to stimuli. This sluggish feeling is only one of many means by which the body signals that it is receiving an unbalanced diet.

Hunger is a condition not of the stomach but of the blood, which sends signals to the brain that the blood needs nutrients. A hungry person may feel slightly restless, irritable, or tense. After a while, the person will experience gnawing feelings—hunger pangs. These pangs are signals sent by the brain, which will also indicate a sensation of thirst when the body's water balance is too low. Eating satisfies hunger, just as drinking satisfies thirst.

Nonetheless, people do not eat only because they need food. They also eat out of habit, tension, or frustration. And although the body demands its daily supply of water, it does not signal that it is deficient in other nutrients. In many cultures, eating is truly a habit. Many people feel hungry at a particular hour simply because they normally eat at that time. A craving for sweets does not mean the person is low in sugar. It is usually the response to a habit to which the body has become conditioned.

By choosing from an assortment of different foods, a person has a good chance of eating foods that contain all the necessary nutrients. A good diet, or eating pattern, must meet all the body's needs—helping the body to keep tissues and organs healthy and functioning properly.

Some people must choose their foods more carefully than others. Diabetics, heart patients, and people with ulcers are among those who must eliminate certain foods from their meals. Unfortunately, the large majority of those who follow specific diets are not looking to improve their nutrition but to find a quick, easy way to lose weight. The newsstands are filled with slick magazines featuring stories about some fabulous new diet discovery. Ads constantly encourage people to "lose 20 pounds in 10 days" or "lose 5 inches in 7 days." The truth is, few fad diets work. Studies show that when people lose weight too quickly, they regain it even more quickly. Moreover, fad diets are as difficult to stick to as old eating habits are to break.

Some people create their own weight-loss diets. This can lead to serious nutritional deficiency. A person who starves all day and then eats one big meal at dinnertime will not lose weight, even if he or she is eating the right foods. An overworked digestive system cannot easily handle an oversupply of food. The consequence is that the body burns muscle tissue while it stores more fat. The dieter becomes fatter and weaker while taking in fewer calories than ever.

Most "miracle" diets require people to depart radically from their normal eating routines, a change that can slow down metabolism, the rate at which the body conducts its chemical activities. Once the diet ends, the body continues to burn fuel slowly, and even normal eating leads to weight gain.

There are healthy ways to lose weight. They usually involve learning a new way of eating. All diets should be planned under the supervision of a doctor or a nutritionist, who will make sure the person is eating well-balanced meals that provide all the necessary nutrients. The dieter's health should be regularly monitored for any sign of adverse side effects. It is important to understand that there is no universal weight-loss diet. A truly effective diet is one planned specifically for the individual person, one that does not sacrifice his or her long-term well-being for the sake of a few unwanted pounds.

Good digestion is determined by what and how a person eats. The human body needs an adequate amount of all the necessary nutrients every day. Therefore, a balanced diet must contain carbohydrates, proteins, fats, vitamins, minerals, and water. Each of the trillions of cells that make up the body need materials for the constant release of energy and for ongoing growth and repair.

The best way to help the digestive system function efficiently is to eat in as relaxed an atmosphere as possible. Choose your foods carefully from as wide a variety as you can find. Try not to eat too much at any one time, and never eat more food in a day than your body can comfortably handle. Too much food puts a strain on the digestive system, and your body will signal its distress. A healthy system tells you when you have had enough.

Chew your food well. Remember that digestion begins in your mouth, where softening, grinding, cutting, and tearing are methods of assisting your stomach. Meals should include roughage— such as unpeeled fruit, lightly cooked or steamed vegetables, and bran. The roughage from these foods does not get digested but keeps your large intestine in good order.

Do not drink too much with meals. Liquids can dilute the digestive juices and make digestion more difficult. Liquids can also dissolve many water-soluble vitamins and minerals that then get washed out of the system in urine. Do not hurry your meals; the digestive system should remain calm and relaxed during the complicated tasks it must perform.

Most digestion in the body is carried on without your assistance. Nevertheless, you do play a vital part in helping the digestive system to work properly and effectively. An understanding of the digestive system and the things that may affect it equips you to keep it healthy and in good condition.

APPENDIX

FOR MORE INFORMATION

GENERAL INFORMATION

American Liver Foundation
1425 Pompton Avenue
Cedar Grove, NJ 07009
800-223-0179
973-857-2626
www.liverfoundation.org

Provides counseling, self-help groups, and information about liver disorders

Iron Overload Diseases Association, Inc.
433 Westwind Drive
North Palm Beach, FL 33408
561-840-8512
www.iod.ironoverload.org

Provides information and medical referrals and sponsors conferences to hemochromatosis victims and their families

National Digestive Disease Education and Information Clearinghouse
Two Information Way
Bethesda, MD 20892
301-654-3810
www.niddk.nih.gov

Hepatitis Foundation, Intl.
30 Sunrise Terrace
Cedar Grove, NJ
973-239-1035
www.hepfi.org

National Foundation for Ileitis and Colitis
386 Park Avenue South
New York, NY 10016
800-932-2423
www.ccfa.org

A research organization dedicated to finding the cause of and cure for ileitis and colitis

United Ostomy Association
36 Executive Park, Suite 120
Irvine, CA 92714
800-826-0826
www.uoa.org

Mutual aid, moral support, and education for people with colostomy or ileostomy surgery

American Society of Abdominal Surgeons
675 Main Street
Melrose, MA 02176
781-665-6102
www.abdominalsurg.org

Provides information about causes of and treatment for peptic ulcers

Digestive Disease National Coalition
507 Capitol Court NE, Suite 200
Washington, DC 20002
202-544-7497

Provides information about digestive diseases and related nutrition

Gastrointestinal Pathology Club
Dept. of Pathology
St. Barnabas Medical Center
94 Old Shorts Hill Road
Livingston, NJ 07039
973-533-5700

Disseminates information about the pathology of the gastrointestinal tract

American College of Nutrition
302 E. 19th Street
New York, NY 10003-2895
212-777-1037
www.am-coll-nutr.org

Educates the public about clinical and
experimental developments in the field of
nutrition

The International Foundation for
   Functional Gastrointestinal Disorders
www.execpc.com/iffgd

U.S. Food and Drug Administration
Office of Consumer Affairs
5600 Fishers Lane
Rockville, MD 20857
301-827-4420
www.fda.gov

CENTERS FOR DIGESTIVE DISEASE RESEARCH

ALABAMA
Gastroenterology Division
University of Alabama at Birmingham
LHR 404
University Station
Birmingham, AL 35294
205-934-6060

ARIZONA
Gastroenterology Division
University of Arizona College of Medicine
Arizona Health Sciences Center
1501 N. Campbell Avenue
Tucson, AZ 85724
520-694-0111
www.medicine.arizona.edu/
   gastroenterology/

ARKANSAS
Gastroenterology Division
University of Arkansas College of Medicine
4301 W. Markham Street, Slot 567
Little Rock, AR 72205
501-686-7000
www.uams.edu

COLORADO
Gastroenterology Section
University of Colorado Health Sciences,
   University Hospital
4200 E. 9th Ave.
Denver, CO 80262
303-372-0000
www.uchsc.edu/uh

CONNECTICUT
Department of Internal Medicine
Yale University School of Medicine
333 Cedar Street
New Haven, CT 06510
203-785-4672
info.med.yale.edu/intmed/

DISTRICT OF COLUMBIA
Gastroenterology Division
George Washington University
Medical Center
2150 Pennsylvania Avenue, NW
Washington, D.C. 20007
202-994-4112
www.gwumc.edu

FLORIDA
Gastroenterology Division
University of Florida College of
   Medicine
1600 SW Archer Road, #HD602
PO Box J-214
Gainesville, FL 32610
352-392-2877
www.ufl.edu

GEORGIA
Gastroenterology Division
Emory University School of
   Medicine
69 Butler Street
Atlanta, GA 30303
404-616-6817

ILLINOIS

Section of Gastroenterology
University of Chicago Medical Center
Michael Reese Hospital and Medical Center
5841 S. Maryland Avenue
Chicago, IL 60637
312-791-2000

INDIANA

Gastroenterology Section
Department of Medicine
Indiana University Medical Center
University Hospital N541
926 West Michigan Street
Indianapolis, IN 46223
317-274-5000
www.iupui.edu

IOWA

Gastroenterology Section
University of Iowa Hospitals & Clinics
200 Hawkins Dr.
Iowa City, IA 52242
319-335-3500
www.uiowa.edu

KANSAS

Department of Medicine
University of Kansas College of Health
   Sciences
3901 Rainbow Blvd.
Kansas City, KS 66103
913-588-5000
www.gastro.org

KENTUCKY

University of Kentucky Medical Center
Department of Medicine, GI Division
Room MN 654
Lexington, KY 45036
606-323-8586
www.mccs.uky.edu

LOUISIANA

Gastroenterology Division
Tulane University School of Medicine
1430 Tulane Avenue
New Orleans, LA 70112
504-588-5412

MARYLAND

Gastroenterology Section
Johns Hopkins Hospital
600 N. Wolfe Street
Baltimore, MD 21205
410-955-5000
www.med.jhu.edu/jhhr/

MASSACHUSETTS

Department of Medicine
Harvard Medical School
Massachusetts General Hospital
55 Fruit Street
Boston, MA 02114
617-726-2000
www.partners.org

MICHIGAN

Gastroenterology Division
University of Michigan Medical Center
3952 Taubman Building
1500 E. Medical Ctr. Dr.
Ann Arbor, MI 48109
734-764-5944
www.med.umich.edu

MINNESOTA

Gastroenterology Section
Mayo Clinic–Mayo Medical School
200 First Street, SW
Rochester, MN 55905
507-284-2511
www.mayo.edu

MISSISSIPPI

Department of Digestive Diseases
University of Mississippi Medical Center
2500 North State Street
Jackson, MS 39216
601-984-1145
www.umsmed.edu

MISSOURI

Gastroenterology Division
Washington University School of Medicine
660 S. Euclid
St. Louis, MO 63110
314-747-3000
www.bjc.org

NEBRASKA

Gastroenterology Division
Creighton University School of
    Medicine
2500 Cal. Plaza
Omaha, NE 68178
402-280-2700
www.creighton.edu

NEW HAMPSHIRE

Gastroenterology Division
Dartmouth Medical School
Hitchcock Clinic
1 Medical Ctr. Dr.
Lebanon, NH 03756-0001
603-650-5000
www.Hitchcock.org

NEW JERSEY

Gastroenterology Division
University of Medicine & Dentistry
    of N.J.
100 Bergen Street
Newark, NJ 07103
973-972-4300
www.umdnj.edu

NEW MEXICO

Division of Gastroenterology
Department of Medicine
University of New Mexico School of
    Medicine
Albuquerque, NM 87131
505-272-2610
www.unm.edu

NEW YORK

Digestive Diseases Research Center
Albert Einstein College of Medicine
1300 Morris Park Avenue, #-G42
Bronx, NY 10461
718-904-2000

NORTH CAROLINA

Division of Digestive Disease & Nutrition
778 Burnett-Womack Building
University of North Carolina
Chapel Hill, NC 27514
919-962-2211
www.med.unc.edu/ibs

OHIO

Division of Gastroenterology
Case Western Reserve University School
    of Medicine
Cleveland Metropolitan General Hospital
2119 Abington Road
Cleveland, OH 44106
216-368-2000
www.cwru.edu

OKLAHOMA

Digestive Diseases and Nutrition
The University of Oklahoma Health
    Sciences Center
PO Box 26307
Oklahoma City, OK 73126
405-271-5428
www.ouhsc.edu

OREGON

Gastroenterology Division
Oregon Health Sciences University
    School of Medicine
3181 S.W. Sam Jackson Park Road
Portland, OR 97201
503-494-8577

PENNSYLVANIA

Gastroenterology Division
The Medical College of Pennsylvania
3300 Henry Avenue
Philadelphia, PA 19129
215-842-6000
www.tenethealth.com

PUERTO RICO

Gastroenterology Division
University of Puerto Rico
Medical Sciences Campus
School of Medicine
GPO Box 5067
San Juan, PR 00936
809-754-3649

SOUTH CAROLINA

Dept. of Med. Gastroenterology and
   Metabolism Division
University of South Carolina
School of Medicine
96 Jonatha Lucas Street
Charlston, SC 29425
843-792-2081
www.musc.edu

SOUTH DAKOTA

Division of Gastroenterology
Department of Medicine
University of South Dakota
School of Medicine
1400 West 22nd Street
Sioux Falls, SD 57105
605-357-1300
www.usd.edu

TENNESSEE

Gastroenterology Division
Vanderbilt University Medical School
D3300 Medical Center North
Nashville, TN 37232-2104
615-322-2164
www.mc.vander.edu/medschool

TEXAS

Gastroenterology Division
University of Texas Health Science Center
   at Houston
6431 Fannin Street, Rm. G.010
Houston, TX 77030
713-500-5010
www.med.uth.tmc.edu

UTAH

Gastroenterology Division
University of Utah School of Medicine
50 N. Medical Drive
Salt Lake City, UT 84132
801-581-7802
www.med.utah.edu/gi

VERMONT

Gastroenterology Division
Department of Medicine
University of Vermont
Given Building Room C-317
Burlington, VT 05405
802-656-1414
www.uvm.edu

WASHINGTON

Gastroenterology Division
University of Washington School of
   Medicine, RG-24
Seattle, WA 98195
206-548-2888
www.washington.edu

WEST VIRGINIA

Gastroenterology Division
Marshall University School of Medicine
400 Hal Greer Blvd.
Huntingon, WV 25755
304-696-3170
www.marshall.edu

WISCONSIN

Gastroenterology Division
University of Wisconsin Medical School
Department of Medicine
600 Highland Avenue, J5/235
608-263-8000
www.uwhospital.org

APPENDIX

FURTHER READING

American Cancer Society. *Cancer Facts and Figures—1994*. Atlanta: American Cancer Society, 1995.

Berkow, Robert (ed). *The Merck Manual of Medical Information*. West Point, PA: Merck & Co., 1997.

Bolt, Robert J. *Digestive System*. New York: John Wiley, 1983.

Galambos, John T., and Theodore Hersh, eds. *Digestive Diseases*. Stoneham, MA: Butterworth, 1997.

Gossel, Thomas A., and Donald W. Stansloski. *The Complete Medicine Book*. New York: Crescent Books, 1995.

Kirschmann, Gayla. *Nutrition Almanac*, 4th ed. New York: McGraw-Hill, 1996.

Levin, Bernard. *The Amercian Cancer Society: Colorectal Cancer*. New York: Random House, 1999.

Memmler, R. *The Human Body in Health and Disease*, 7th ed. Philadelphia, Lippincott, 1992.

Marieb, E. N. *Human Anatomy and Physiology*, 3rd ed. Redwood City, CA: Benjamin Cummings, 1995.

Mylander, Maureen. *The Great American Stomach Book*. New York: Ticknor and Fields, 1992.

National Research Council, Food and Nutrition Board. *Recommended Dietary Allowances*, 10th ed. Washington, D.C.: National Academy Press, 1989.

Natow, Annette, and Jo-Ann Heslin. *The Pocket Encyclopedia of Nutrition*. New York: Pocket Books, 1997.

Reynolds, Moira S. *The Outstretched Hand: Modem Medical Discoveries*. New York: Richards Rosen, 1980.

Smith, Anthony. *The Body*. New York: Viking, 1986.

Specter, Steven (ed). *Viral Hepatitis: Diagnosis, Therapy, and Prevention*. Louisville: Humana, 1999.

Thomas, Clayton L. (ed.). *Taber's Cyclopedia Medical Dictionary*, 18th ed. Philadelphia: F. A. Davis, 1997.

Thompson, W. *Ulcer Story*. New York: Plenum, 1996.

Wurtman, Judith. *Managing Your Mind and Mood Through Food*. New York: Rawson, 1987.

GLOSSARY

Alimentary canal: The digestive tube extending from the mouth to the anus; includes mouth, pharynx, esophagus, stomach, and small and large intestines.

Amino acid: Any one of a number of organic compounds containing an amino group and a carboxyl group; the fundamental building block of proteins.

Amylase: A digestive enzyme found in salivary and pancreatic juices.

Anus: The outlet of the rectum.

Appendix: An appendage attached to the cecum portion of the colon.

Bile: A secretion of the liver that aids digestion, especially the emulsification and absorption of fats.

Bolus: A lump of chewed food ready to be swallowed.

Carbohydrate: A member of a group of organic compounds that share a general biochemical structure of carbon, hydrogen, and oxygen; sugars and starches are carbohydrates.

Cholesterol: A waxy fatlike substance produced in the liver or ingested in the form of saturated fats.

Chyme: Food mixed with stomach chemicals, expelled by the stomach into the duodenum.

Cirrhosis: Fibrosis, or hardening, of the liver; often the result of chronic alcoholism.

Colitis: Inflammation of the colon.

Colon: The main part of the large intestine.

Colostomy: A surgical opening from the colon to outside the body.

Constipation: Difficult or infrequent elimination of feces from the body.

Diarrhea Abnormally frequent intestinal evacuation, usually marked by soft or watery stools.

Duodenum: The first part of the small intestine.

Emulsify: To separate fats into small globules that remain suspended in the fluid food mass.

Endoscope: Instrument that can be used for viewing the alimentary canal.

Enzyme: A member of a group of proteins that are produced by a living cell and trigger, or catalyze, certain chemical reactions.

Esophagus: Tube that carries food from the throat to the stomach.

Fat: A substance containing one or more fatty acids; the main substance into which excess carbohydrates are converted for storage by the human body.

Feces: Solid or semisolid waste products of digestion eliminated through the anus.

Fistula: An abnormal passageway often formed by infection or injury.

Fundus: The base of a hollow organ; the greater curvature of the stomach, bordering on the esophagus.

Gallbladder: A muscular sac in which bile from the liver is stored.

Gastrectomy: The surgical removal of all or part of the stomach.

Gastroenteritis: Inflammation of the stomach lining.

Gingivitis: Inflammation of the gums.

Glucose: A simple six-carbon sugar.

Glycogen: A carbohydrate composed of chains of glucose units; the form in which sugar is stored in the liver.

Hiatal hernia: A condition in which the lower end of the stomach or esophagus protrudes through the diaphragm.

Hepatitis: An infectious disease characterized by inflammation of the liver.

Hydrochloric acid: An acid found in a digestive chemical secreted by the stomach.

Hydrolysis: Process of decomposition involving the splitting of a molecule and the addition of the elements of water.

Ileostomy: A surgical opening from the ileum to outside the body.

Ileum: The last portion of the small intestine; located between the jejunum and the large intestine.

Insulin: A hormone secreted by the pancreas; essential for the metabolism of carbohydrates.

Jaundice: Yellowing of the skin and whites of the eyes; caused by the deposition of bile pigments.

Jejunum: The portion of the small intestine between the duodenum and the ileum.

Large intestine: The final portion of the alimentary canal.

Lipase: A pancreatic enzyme.

Lipid: Member of a group of compounds soluble in certain solvents; this group includes fats.

Liver: Largest gland in the body; aids the digestive process by secreting bile.

Maltose: A sugar composed of two glucose units; the first breakdown of starch digestion.

Metabolize: To change substances chemically within a living organism in order to release useful energy.

Monosaccharide: One of a number of simple sugars sharing the same general formula.

Mucus: Secretion that lubricates organ linings.

Neurotransmitter: A chemical that passes brain messages from cell to cell.

Nutrients: Substances found in food that are essential to bodily function.

Pancreas: The body's second largest gland; secretes insulin, a hormone essential to digestion.

Pepsin: A digestive enzyme secreted by the stomach.

Peristalsis: Muscular movement that pushes food through the alimentary canal.

Portal vein: Vein connecting the small intestine and the liver.

Protein: A complex molecule consisting of a combination of amino acids.

Pylorus: Portion of the stomach that borders on the duodenum.

Rectum: Muscular end of the large intestine.

Renin: Digestive enzyme produced in the stomach; coagulates milk.

Saliva: Digestive juice secreted into the mouth.

Serotonin: Compound found in many body tissues; among other functions it inhibits gastric secretion and serves as a central neurotransmitter.

Small intestine: The part of the intestine that lies between the stomach and colon; the chief site of the absorption of digested nutrients.

Sphincter: Muscle that opens and closes bodily openings.

Trypsin: A protein-digesting enzyme.

Villi: Fingerlike projections that line the small intestine and other membranous surfaces.

Ulcer: An open sore caused by a break in the mucous membrane or the skin.

APPENDIX

INDEX

APPENDIX

PICTURE CREDITS

Regina Avraham has been a science teacher with the New York City Board of Education since the 1960s. She also edits and writes textbooks and general-interest books for young adults. She is the author of *The Circulatory System* in the Chelsea House ENCYCLOPEDIA OF HEALTH and *The Downside of Drugs* in the Chelsea House ENCYCLOPEDIA OF PSYCHOACTIVE DRUGS SERIES 2. Ms. Avraham currently teaches biology and coordinates a science magnet program in New York City.

C. Everett Koop, M.D., Sc.D., currently serves as chairman of the board of his own website, www.drkoop.com, and is the Elizabeth DeCamp McInerny professor at Dartmouth College, from which he graduated in 1937. Dr. Koop received his doctor of medicine degree from Cornell Medical College in 1941 and his doctor of science degree from the University of Pennsylvania in 1947. A pediatric surgeon of international reputation, he was previously surgeon in chief of Children's Hospital of Philadelphia and professor of pediatric surgery and pediatrics at the University of Pennsylvania. A former U.S. Surgeon General, Dr. Koop was also the director of the Office of International Health. He has served as surgery editor of the *Journal of Clinical Pediatrics* and editor in chief of the *Journal of Pediatric Surgery*. In his more than 60 years of experience in health care, government, and industry, Dr. Koop has received numerous awards and honors, including 35 honorary degrees.